And the Cricket was Good Too!

by
Paul Duffin

Cover design by Claire Duffin

©2017 Paul Duffin

PREFACE

Losing most of my sight and hearing, leaving me classified as severely impaired has led to a lot of changes in my life. The cause of the inflammation inside my head is unknown. It has been a progression, which started with losing most of the vision in my left eye at the end of 2001. At the time this was my good eye as the vision in my right eye failed to fully develop from birth, due to the late discovery of a squint. The sight in my right eye has continued to slowly deteriorate. My hearing started to deteriorate in 2010 and my deafness is now profound in my left ear and severe in the right.

The first major impact was retiring in 2002 at the age of 48 years. I remember one consultant telling me to prepare for a new way of life. I did, and am still doing so. The losses to my way of life have steadily mounted. Not surprisingly driving was the first to go ending abruptly. As my hearing deteriorated the cinema and theatre were no longer visited. I used to enjoy the radio, but this is now impossible and I have not heard any music for some time. Conversation is limited to one to one away from noisy environments and also excludes the use of the telephone. Group situations are a real trial and are mostly avoided. I particularly regret not being able to explain to my young grandson why I cannot understand what he is saying to me. I have also lost all sense of smell due to a biopsy through my nose in 2014. This in turn has affected my ability to taste.

This all sounds terrible BUT remarkably, the human spirit is extremely robust and I still feel alive and able to contribute. Adapt and survive is therefore my motto. I can still be taken to enjoy cricket, albeit with the aid of a powerful pair of binoculars. I can also still write with the aid of my large Apple Mac computer

I turned to writing in 2015 and self published on Amazon in November 2016. My first book, Not Too Bad (NTB) is light hearted and based on the diaries I kept from the start of my O' level year in 1970 to the end of 1974 when I started work at the Leeds Permanent Building Society. All the proceeds from NTB have gone to Guide dogs. I soon passed my target of 200 sales and £1000 for the charity.

I really enjoyed both the writing and the feedback from readers. I decided to base this second book on my nine cricket tours following the England team around the world. I had a good starting point as during the last five tours I had sent home a blog. I had also kept a diary on the first trip to Australia. Being a bit of a hoarder, I had also retained a lot of the tour details supplied by the three different tour companies. You will probably notice the difference between the first half and the latter tours.

All the sale proceeds (royalties) from this book will go to Sense (www.sense.org.uk) a charity that supports people who like me have both sight and hearing loss. I discovered them whilst researching for NTB. The first solicitor I shared a room with at Wragge & Co in Birmingham was a chap called John Crabtree. It turned out that after a very successful career at Wragges, amongst his many current roles he is Chairman of Sense.

Writing has given me a very rewarding outlet, that hopefully will contribute a small amount to other people with similar issues and also provide an enjoyable read to many.

At this point I must thank my two wonderful assistants who have provided excellent editorial guidance and support, Liz Lavender and Andy Bates. I really could not have done this without them. The cover has been designed by my talented daughter, Claire Duffin.

I am also grateful to the help given by Colin Weaver, who I shared two tours with, John Peck and Richard Birchall three tours and my main cricket buddy Stuart Rhodes, four tours.

Finally, I must thank my wife Sue and other family and friends who have had to put up with my constant references to "my book".

Paul Duffin
November 2017

INTRODUCTION

I have always been interested in cricket, from my very earliest days of playing catch in the garden with my Dad and brother Steve back in Yardley, Birmingham. Later, I spent hour upon hour hitting a tennis ball along the drive between our house and our neighbours, the Beresford's. A good shot would be over the road into the Tranters' front garden and rewarded with four runs.

As a youngster my hero was Ted Dexter, which led me to follow the fortunes of Sussex CCC even though as a Brummie my local team was Warwickshire CCC. My brother Steve and I had many games of "howzat" the cricket dice game. I would be Sussex and Steve would be Warwickshire. Many hours of fun with no screens in sight.

My Dad (Stan Duffin) was a useful cricketer and all round sportsman, benefitting from being ambidextrous. This enabled him to use both hands when playing tennis, serving with one and playing ground strokes with the other. On the cricket field he bowled with his left arm and batted right handed. He was eventually awarded honorary life membership at Warwickshire CCC for his support of local cricket, particularly when he was secretary of the Birmingham Cooperative Sports club based in Barrows Lane, Yardley.

Tragically my Dad suffered a fatal heart attack at the age of forty eight when I was just fifteen. He had been a great support to me and my school, Central Grammar, where I opened the batting and captained the side in my first three years. I went on to play for the first and second eleven but my scores diminished along with my eyesight. I only discovered my visual weakness when I started to learn to drive a car, as opposed to a cricket ball.

After I left school, playing cricket was limited to work teams playing 20 over games for fun. We all had to bowl 2 overs and retire if we scored 25. I was never attracted to weekend club cricket, due mainly to the time commitment, as, after joining the Leeds Permanent Building Society in 1974, I had to work most Saturday mornings.

I have always enjoyed watching cricket, both on TV and live matches mainly Tests and one day internationals. When I moved to Wetherby, I became a member of Yorkshire CCC at Headingly, which has led to my enjoyment of many county matches.

Apart from watching Yorkshire I like to meet up with old friends from Birmingham, including Paul Thomson, Stuart Hardie, John Stoker, Martin Wood, Rob Miles and Pete Olive. This has led to visits to the Cheltenham and Scarborough Cricket festivals and matches at Worcester and Edgbaston, all very enjoyable. Even a trip to Chesterfield was good fun where, due to a waterlogged pitch not a ball was bowled in our three day stay.

I am also lucky to have my friend Stuart Rhodes who takes me to the grounds and has accompanied me on several of my tours abroad.

After my sight problems forced me to retire in 2002 I decided to travel. I took two of my offspring, Steve and Claire, on a tour of the west coast of America. It was so enjoyable it encouraged me to accept an invitation to travel with a friend to Australia and the cricket tours were launched.

The tours were very different, and the chapters vary in detail due the records I kept. These varied from a brief diary for Chapter One to the blogs I sent home that formed the basis for the last four chapters. The tour of India is recalled almost entirely from my memories and those of my friend Colin Weaver. The main impact is the appearance of far more characters in the second half of the book

A couple of the tales are to some extent at the expense of one or two individuals. They are told accurately, and their identities have been protected. No harm intended.

CHAPTER 1 AUSTRALIA January 2003

Of the nine England cricket tours I have experienced this is the only one that wasn't an organised cricket tour. It is therefore very different from the other eight. Later tours will see the emergence of several interesting characters and their amusing tales and events. My trip to Australia in 2003 was just my friend Rick and I but was still eventful as you are about to find out.

THE COUNTRY

There are lots of things we all know about Australia. For a start, it's a long way from the UK. From my home in Wetherby, West Yorkshire it is more than 10,500 miles. It is also big! In fact, twenty four times the size of Britain and not much smaller than the USA. The coastline stretches for an amazing 22800 miles. It is however fairly flat with the highest point just 2228ms (7300ft) above sea level. The population is c24 million, 88% of whom live in urban areas.

What is not so well known is that the reputation of spiders and other creepy crawlers as big killers is exaggerated, being more fear than fact. The last recorded fatality following a spider bite was in 2016 but you would have to go right back to 1981 for the previous fatal incident involving the little blighters. The biggest killer 'down under', after humans of course, is the horse with 77 people falling prey to equine incidents in the last decade. Crocodiles actually account for, on average, less than one fatality a year. Safe to go then!

50 NOT OUT

A trip to the other side of the world was definitely not on my immediate agenda when I finally retired from HBOS in October 2002 due to problems with my sight. Then my good friend Rick Firth informed me that his plan to visit

Australia to celebrate his fiftieth birthday the following January with his wife Pam had very unfortunately been thrown into disarray due to his father-in-law's serious illness.

"Would you be interested in taking Pam's place?" he asked.
"Are bears catholic?" I quickly replied, mixing my metaphors somewhat (in the woods and the Pope).

"We will have to share a room on occasions". In the interest of keeping costs down I readily agreed. We were long standing friends and I naturally thought nothing of it at the time. However, my view changed rapidly after our first shared night in Sydney, as you will soon discover.

When it came to the itinerary, Rick was also very keen to see some cricket during the trip and planned to take in England's final Ashes Test of the five match series. However due to the traditional test ground allocation and proximity to the New Year we would not be able to see all five days. We hoped the match would still be alive when we arrived for the last two days of scheduled play. It was Rick's celebration and he was in charge of the itinerary, so the plan was fine by me.

BUSINESS CLASS AT A PREMIUM

My only request was for me to be in business class on such a long journey. Rick found what appeared to be a really good deal with Thai Airways. On boarding it soon became clear that this was not the business class I was expecting. There was no flat bed just a big seat, admittedly with plenty of leg room, but it was really more like premium economy, or business deficit.

24 HOURS IN BANGKOK

To break the journey we stopped over for twenty four hours in Bangkok. We booked into the very pleasant Landmark Hotel and went straight to the bar for an extremely welcome Singha beer or two before heading down to the famous - or should I say infamous – Patpong Night Market.

Rick had visited Bangkok before and was more familiar with the locals than me. As we wandered the streets and entered the bars he repeatedly challenged me to sort the "lady boys" from the girls. He hinted that the two main giveaways were foot size and the presence of an Adam's apple. Sounds simple enough to spot the difference but it wasn't that easy. I found the bar atmosphere a little intimidating, particularly when the hosts were keen to approach and sit on my lap. Well girls will be girls… but were they really? I soon decided the best strategy was to adopt a firm rebuff and when this didn't work we abandoned beer and bars in favour of the market and designer fakes.

Bangkok is a strange city with its modern monorail running through ancient buildings. Western shops such as Boots and Body Shop were prevalent as were many designer outlets. Strangely, and somewhat alarmingly, we came across a baby elephant being paraded in the street to raise money. The poor thing did not look at all happy or particularly healthy. We both felt this should not be allowed but no one seemed to bat an eyelid.

The next morning Rick informed me that he had planned a comprehensive tour of the city's main attractions. We hired a car for several hours (a man with a Merc'). He dropped us off at the Chao Phraya River where we boarded a Long Tail speedboat: an unusual craft with the propeller at the end of a long driveshaft. The fumes were pungent, but the power was impressive. We shot down the main river and eventually entered a quieter stretch next to the flower market. The man with the Merc' was very conveniently waiting for us downstream.

We went on to visit the Grand Palace. A spectacular 250 year old building. The former home of the King and government had a strict dress code on entering the temple section, which caught a few tourists but not us Brits. We had just enough time to make it to the airport for our flight to Sydney.

AT HOME DOWN UNDER

I had a very strange feeling when leaving the airport in Sydney as I immediately felt at home. Some describe Australia as a cross between England and America, which is a pretty good way to view it. Our hotel was very close to Circular Quay from where the ferryboats dock and depart all day long. From there we headed straight to Doyle's, the famous fish restaurant, for a very pleasant lunch before setting off to wander the city and establish our bearings. That night we were 'fortunate' enough to experience our first Aussie pub and taste a pint of local beer, Victoria Bitter aka VB. Firstly it is not a bitter, it is in fact a lager; secondly it is not a pint as we know it. An Aussie pint is about three quarters of a UK pint (15floz). Having said that it tastes ok, if a little weak.

TWENTY YEAR SECRET REVEALED

Back at the hotel Rick and I stumbled into our shared twin room. After an exhausting couple of days, I quickly succumbed to blissful sleep but was alarmed when my peace was broken by an unfamiliar sound. I quickly located the source and realised it was Rick snoring. But this was no ordinary nocturnal snuffle this was Olympic snoring! I was forced to take action. My first strategy was to stick my leg out from the covers and gently nudge his bed. The joggle woke Rick enough for him to turn over and peace returned. However, my success was short lived as it turns out that Rick was able to recommence snoring even though he was now face down in the pillow. Strategy two was for a second, more violent, bed-shifting nudge to be dealt. This worked momentarily but the snoring soon recommenced. I continued nudging for a while but eventually gave up. A disturbed night followed.

When Rick woke up he found his bed had moved several feet and was now located under the window. I awoke to a baffled Rick exclaiming, "How did I get here!" I provided a detailed and somewhat weary explanation and Rick looked at me aghast "But I don't snore" he protested vehemently. "If I did Pam would have told me". Pam was his wife of nearly 20 years at the time of the trip. Eager to set the matter straight Rick immediately rang Pam and passed me the phone. Not wishing to be the instigator of marital disharmony, I rather reluctantly asked the question, and Pam, somewhat sheepishly, confirmed the truth: Rick is indeed an Olympian snorer. Her simple defence was that she hadn't had the heart to tell him and had just put up with it...for years. With evident reluctance Rick accepted the truth. I was pleased the truth had been revealed but was already dreading the next night...

TESTING TIMES

England had already lost the previous four Test matches and therefore the five match series was effectively over as a contest. However, England players and supporters alike considered this to be an opportunity to restore some pride. The first three days had gone some way towards that goal. Australia were just one run ahead after the first innings. As we arrived at the Sydney Cricket Ground (the SCG) for the start of the fourth day, England were 218 for 2 with Michael Vaughan 113 not out. Vaughan went on to score a superb 183, and Hussain secured 72. At the end of play Australia were 91 for 3.

The tables had turned. We were beginning to think we could win.

The SCG wasn't full which made it easy for Rick and I to move around and mix with the Barmy Army on the famous Hill, where it was rumoured that the beer was at half strength to try and limit their exuberance. It also gave us the opportunity to experience the different parts of the historic stadium.

An interesting addition to the beer provision was the appearance of the "beer wenches". The young girls could be hired for $65 an hour to fetch and carry drinks. Hardly child labour at these prices but I doubt they were paid anything like the cost. We didn't hire their services but they were certainly a colourful addition to the cricket. All in all, it was a jolly good day, followed by a slap up meal that night in the lively and entertaining Darling Harbour area.

We returned to the ground for the final day and YIPPEE we did it. England won by 225 runs with Caddick taking 7 for 94. Great stuff, so exciting, and we were there!

The total attendance for all five days was recorded as 181,778, with a 20,652 strong crowd on the last day. This was Australia's first home defeat for four years. The absence, due to injury, of both McGrath (side strain) and Warne (shoulder) certainly helped us, but this was a hard fought and much deserved victory. Caddick took ten wickets in the match for the first and last time on what turned out to be his final Test appearance.

We walked back to the hotel via Kings Cross, an area that has much in common with its English namesake. It even has a railway station, albeit on a more modest scale and with only two platforms (and definitely no Harry Potter platform). That night we celebrated with a meal in the Harbour Rocks area, where we were due to stay on our return to Sydney in a week's time.

VERY MANLY

The location of our hotel led us to 'ride the ferries' from Circular Quay. We opted to head for Manly, a beach area about seven miles away. During our half hour ferry journey, we were treated to great views of the Opera House and the Sydney Harbour Bridge. We also passed the building where Michael Parkinson had an apartment. Rumour has it that the locals were not impressed with the property design, consequently dubbing it "the toaster" which seemed very apt. We enjoyed Manly. Strolling along the pleasant front and consuming a compulsory ice cream plus of course the odd beer.

TICK IN THE BOX

Being Brits abroad we decided that it would be remiss of us not to see a performance at the Sydney Opera House. We didn't really care what was on, as long as we could tick the SOH box.

Consequently, that evening we took our ($95) seats in box W47. When I say 'box' I mean one of the many areas segmented by 3ft high wooden boards. We settled down to enjoy La Pasion Segun San Marcos (St Mark's Passion apparently) penned by the Argentinian composer Golijov. I am sure he is very well known in Argentina! Not surprisingly it was performed in Spanish and could have been so much more entertaining if I had spotted the English score translation displayed above the stage. Rick helpfully pointed it out.... at the very end of the performance. I'm not sure how he had followed it though as he had slept through most of it. To be fair to Rick he managed to avoid snoring, there was just a lot of nodding and twitching. Perhaps not our most entertaining evening, but a tick in the Aussie tourist box so to speak.

Note to anyone with a similar desire to tick Sydney boxes: the Opera House is definitely more impressive from the outside.

LIFE'S A BEACH

If you go to Sydney you have to set foot on Bondi Beach, so the very next morning we did just that. Bondi is only a short drive from Sydney and, having missed out the previous day, Rick was keen to try out our newly acquired wheels.

Unfortunately, our expectations, fuelled by the hype, weren't fully met. Yes, it is a nice beach, but other than that it is not particularly impressive. Visitors should prepare to be underwhelmed by the 1950s style changing rooms. After a short stay admiring the beach and its inhabitants, we turned our attention to lunch and strolled along the front looking for a suitable venue. Rick spotted a building with an impressive balcony overlooking the beach and declared that this was the place. We made our way to the ground floor entrance to discover that it was actually the "Ex- Servicemen's Club: North Bondi Returned and Services League". In other words, the Australian equivalent of our British Legion Club. Not being ex-servicemen, we questioned our eligibility but quickly discovered that as we lived well outside the area we could apply for temporary membership. We duly did, and within minutes we were in and delighted to discover good food, cheap drinks and oddly, an in-house betting area which could be found in most RSL clubs. We only took advantage of the first two and made our way on to the balcony to savour the great views. We loved it.

ON THE ROAD TO BRISBANE

We left Sydney, departing over the Harbour Bridge, to begin our long drive to Brisbane where, after a one-night stop over, we would fly to Hamilton Island, part of the Whitsunday Islands. We made our first stop at a winery in the Hunter Valley. Not surprisingly we immediately joined a 'local' wine tasting tour, although strangely all the wines we tasted came from outside the area. Not that we were deterred.

Now that we were out of the big city the accommodation was a little more basic and I began to treat every single insect as a potential killer. The swimming pool was definitely off limits for me but not for Rick who was keen to get full value from our stop.

The next day we were back on the road heading north. It soon became clear that the main road from Sydney to Brisbane has little to offer by way of interesting views. The sides of the road were banked with bushes and trees that you can't see beyond. It's all pretty monotonous. We did however enjoy lunch at Port Macquarie, before motoring on to our next overnight stop.

Coffs Harbour is famous for being the home of New Zealand born film star Russell Crowe (cousin of the cricketing Crowe brothers). For us it became memorable for the wind. As we got out of the car it was blowing so hard we could lean right into it and not fall over. This entertained us for a while after our long journey! Rick had booked a nice apartment that we found easily and then headed to the yacht club for something to eat. This was followed by a quick visit to the fun fair, and we finished off the night listening to a pretty good live band that we found in a local bar. Coffs Harbour also claims fame for the 'Big Banana' theme park. On our way out of town the next morning we drove past it. We knew it was there because outside there was a .... "Yes! A Big Banana!" Needless to say, we sped onwards.

Our last stop before reaching Brisbane was Byron Bay. Located approximately 100 miles south of Brisbane it is notable as a former hippy "hang out" and usually a perfect place to stop for lunch. When we arrived, however, we experienced the first rainfall of the trip. It positively poured down. We wisely drove on.

TUMBLING DICE

Eventually we arrived in the pleasant modern sub-tropical city of Brisbane and checked into the excellent Treasury Hotel on the banks of the Brisbane River opposite the Southbank Parklands. Although a former penal colony, Brisbane is now an attractive, flourishing city. We were only staying one night before flying off to Hamilton Island. That evening Rick had arranged to meet a business contact, which meant I had to amuse myself for an hour or two.

The Treasury Casino was next to our hotel. Although not a gambling man it seemed like a good idea to see how long I could make $20 last. I started by having a look round, studied the various options and decided that I would start with blackjack, and if I didn't lose everything straight away, I'd move on to the roulette wheel. It may be the sign of a misspent youth playing cards, but I started pretty well with blackjack. As a teenager I had spent many hours playing cards, with three card brag my game of choice. Try as I may my luck - laced with only a little skill - meant I was still sat at the table over half an hour later. Intending to hang on to my winning streak I decided it was time to move on to the wheel of fortune. I watched it spin for a while before committing any chips. I could not believe what I saw. Zero came up three times in four spins.

I fluctuated between backing a group of four numbers, to simple red or black. By the time I was due to meet Rick I still had not lost, in fact I was slightly up on my $20.

17

Being cautious by nature I resisted the temptation to put the balance on one last bet and left feeling rather good.

TREASURE THIS ISLAND

Although only about a mile square, Hamilton Island is the largest inhabited island of the Whitsundays. Just over 550 miles north of Brisbane the island is a popular tourist destination and we planned to make the most of our three night stay.

It is the only island on the Great Barrier Reef to have its own commercial airport. Jet planes are welcomed, but private cars are banned. The humble golf buggy is the only form of motorised transport. Despite my poor vision, which prevents me from driving at home, I did have a quick go. However, after just a few hair-raising minutes Rick quite rightly took the wheel.

NO BARRIERS

A visit to the Barrier Reef was at the top of our Australia to-do list. As we queued for the boat we were informed that we were likely to encounter a swell of at least six feet and were strongly advised to take advantage of the seasickness tablets being handed out. I duly obliged. We arrived at the floating base after a one hour ride that was choppy but no one was ill as far as we could see. We opted for the optional snorkeling which was very interesting, made more so by the ever present huge grouper fish (I think that's what it was but I am not good on fish unless it is accompanied by mushy peas and chips) who was apparently very much a local resident. He was completely harmless unlike the little blighters that gave Rick a nice bite on his arm. We had a very helpful instructor, which made the experience well worth the extra cost.

As I relaxed in the swell I couldn't help thinking of the two tourists mentioned in Bill Bryson's excellent Down Under book. Somehow, they were left out on the ocean after a diving trip never to be seen again. I made sure I was back on the boat in good time.

HOLD THE LINE

Our second day on the island began with a swing, literally, as we spent the morning on the golf driving range before making our way down to the wharf to board our previously booked speed boat. Rick was keen to have a go at 'proper' sea fishing. This was serious stuff. The kind where you are strapped in to a seat and obliged to wrestle with a very large fish, which, after a long hard fought battle you eventually hope to reel in.

There were seven of us on board, three other paying customers and two crew members. The boat was well equipped and had real power to thrust its way through the waves. The onboard radar was used to search for the prey. It was an exhilarating ride when the throttle was fully open, but a very different story when the engine was cut and we just lolled nauseatingly from side to side. I remembered the advice for such situations was to focus on the horizon. My eyes were glued and my stomach settled, and thank goodness it worked.

After about 30 minutes of lolling one of the crew announced that they had located fish on the radar and our first volunteer was duly strapped to his seat, ready for combat. The battle certainly did commence! The tuna fish on the other end of the line put up a good fight but after a struggle it was reeled in. At the front of our boat there was a large box full of ice intended as the temporary home for our catch. As the tuna exhaled its last breath it was plonked in the box and down went the lid. Dark red blood swilled across the deck, and we were momentarily silenced, reflecting on the catch, but not for long. The tuna had found new life and was banging on the lid with fury. The crewmember stood on top of the box for a while, but when the thrashing tuna continued he eventually resorted to producing his knife and dealing a final blow. Barbaric is the only word to describe these final moments. The whole episode was repeated with a second chap before it was Rick's turn to be strapped in the swiveling seat as I was in no hurry to join the fray.

Rick's battle made the first two look tame. It started well enough, but before too long one of the crew members had to intervene to prevent Rick from being swallowed into the deep, but not before Rick's line almost garroted the poor chap when the tuna fish made a swift left turn. Thankfully he managed to disentangle himself and he and Rick clung on. By now fatigue was taking over and the sweat poured but eventually the two of them won the day and the tuna was landed. The deck was by now a gruesome sea of red blood. I was relieved to hear that we were running out of time and avoided taking my turn in the 'hot' seat. As we docked the three huge tuna fish were presented, photographs were taken and recommendations given to take the fish to a nearby restaurant. We declined, there was no way I could eat the poor things after witnessing their demise.

HEADING FOR THE ROCKS

After an enjoyable and eventful three days on the island we boarded a plane and headed south. The 950 miles back to Sydney took less than two hours. Once back in the city we booked into the Harbour Rocks hotel and the peace of individual rooms. The boutique hotel was an interesting change from our other venues and very well located in the popular Rocks area.

After relaxing and freshening up we set off to meet another of Rick's old friends, John. Despite residing in Oz for some years with his family, he was clearly not

100% sold on the place. We spent an evening listening to him complaining about the complex process he had to endure to become a citizen. Even the way in which the local men drank their beer came under scrutiny. John was definitely not a candidate for the "move to Australia" campaign.

HIGH FLYING BIRTHDAY BOY

The day of Rick's 50th birthday arrived and I had organised a special treat: a helicopter flight over Sydney for us both. I have always found heights a bit of a challenge so opted for the relative safety of the middle seat behind the pilot. Rick had pride of place next to the pilot and also had the only other headset, enabling him to hear the communication between the pilot and the control tower. At times, this was a distinct advantage, like when we made a sudden rapid climb to avoid a seaplane that was landing in the harbour. Rick had heard the pilot's instruction to change altitude; the rest of us just felt a surprising sudden upsurge. It was a spectacular trip over all the main sights of the city and particularly 'exciting' when flying between skyscrapers. The main thing was that Rick enjoyed it.

Our celebrations continued that night as we met up with more of Rick's friends for a dinner cruise around Sydney Harbour. A very pleasant trip and thankfully spent with two very pro Australia "pommies" now resident down under. We rounded off Rick's special day with a few final drinks and turned in with smiles on our faces.

SUITS YOU SIR

Before beginning our homeward journey, we just had time to visit the shops. Rick had spotted that the sales were still on at Moss Bros and we were soon tempted inside. Rick was keen on a new suit and asked the assistant if he could try one on. The assistant enquired as to Rick's waist size, to which Rick confidently responded: "30 inches". The experienced assistance paused and politely came back with: "I think it is a while since sir saw that size" and duly got out his tape measure! He was of course right. The suit was purchased, and Rick was happy although there was a slight suspicion that he had spent his money on a "Ting Tong Wong" rather than a Hugo Boss. He squeezed it into his case and we headed home.

At the end of a great trip I made two decisions; firstly, I was determined to return to Australia and secondly, I was very keen to see more cricket around the world. I would do both.

CHAPTER 2 WEST INDIES March 2004

The success of the trip to Australia with Rick whetted my appetite for more travel. I was keen to follow the England cricket team and decided to try an organised tour. I researched the market and eventually plumped for Gullivers on the grounds that they were experienced sports tour operators, and at the time were rated top for organised cricket tours. Being partially sighted and travelling on my own, the trip was always going to be a bit of a risk but I was very keen to give it a try. The next scheduled winter tour was to the West Indies so I opted for the third and fourth Tests of the series taking place on the islands of Barbados and Antigua.

A couple of weeks before travelling, the Gullivers kit bag arrived. It was stuffed full of goodies including a very smart polo shirt emblazoned with the company logo. That was enough for me; I was all set and good to go. I left home with the strains of Typically Tropical ringing in my ears: "*Oh! We're going to Barbados…*"

BARBADOS

The Caribbean island is quite small. Smaller than the Isle of Man at 21 miles long and stretching only 14 miles across. It's 4200 miles from Wetherby and takes around 9 hours to get there. Despite being remote in distance and attitude it was part of the British Empire from 1627 when it was seized by the British from the Spanish, until it gained independence in 1986.

Barbados has a limited number of claims to fame: it has been the 'spiritual' home of rum since the 17th century; it remains the only country visited by the first US President George Washington; and equally unlikely, it was one of only four scheduled stops for Concorde flights - one of the planes still resides on the island.

Close to 90% of the population are of Afro-Caribbean descent, also known as Bajan. English is the official language, but

Bajan, a sort of English based Creole, is spoken by most of the locals. The majority of tourists to the island are from the UK and the most famous residents are from the world of cricket, namely Sirs Sobers and Walcott.

GETTING SET

I arrived at Gatwick Airport in good time and had a cunning plan to spot other members of our party, "Carnival E" by looking out for people with the Gullivers back pack or polo shirt. I circled Duty Free several times without success then suddenly, Ah Ha! I spotted a familiar logo. But wait a minute, this Gullivers pack was strapped on the back of a lad in his 20's. This couldn't be right, particularly as I had convinced myself that at age 50 I would be one of the younger members of the tour party. I decided not to approach the lad at this stage, and wandered off to re-consider my position as the tour whippersnapper.

As there was no business class on offer I had chosen to pay a little extra and sit up front in the premium seats reckoning that I'd be grateful for the extra legroom on the 9 hour flight. Blow me down, the lad with the bag was sat up front too. I still didn't approach.

The flight was largely uneventful although everything changed when we left the aircraft and entered baggage reclaim. It was chaos! Picture the scene, a small, hot hall heaving with battered bags and crumpled post-flight travellers. There were suitcases and bags everywhere and clearly a distinct lack of organisation.

Eventually, I retrieved my luggage and staggered through to 'Arrivals' where it was a real relief to be met by our tour manager, Margaret Gibson. Peace returned as she soon had us loaded on the coach and we set off on the short drive to our hotel. As well as Margaret, we were extremely fortunate and honoured to have former England cricket captain Mike Denness and his partner Doreen on the trip with us.

Apparently, Mike had recommended our hotel to Gullivers following a previous visit. I had high hopes.

BREEZING IN

The Sea Breeze Hotel was lovely and a good recommendation by Mike. Our home for the next eight nights was situated on the South West coast and had a beautiful private sandy beach. I had a large room with a balcony overlooking the sea, the sound of which rhythmically lulled me to sleep each night. Not that I needed much help that first night after a long journey and a couple of obligatory 'get-to-know-each-other' beers.

There were 31 of us on the tour plus, of course, Margaret, Mike and Doreen. They seemed a pretty good crowd with at least six or seven of us travelling as singles. I soon discovered that the lad with the bag was called James. In order to avoid the penal single supplement, he was sharing a room with a chap called Colin. This arrangement was organised by Gullivers. My fear of being with a group of young lads was quickly allayed as apart from James, I was at the younger end of the age spectrum. James's roommate Colin was old enough to be his Dad and initially didn't appear to be totally happy with his "roomy". Perhaps they were the only ones that asked for sharing. Apparently, James's father had paid for his trip, which explained why he looked a little out of place.

The hotel was quite small and the dining area opened out on both sides to verandas and spectacular views of the ocean. It was lovely to have a welcome breeze drift gently through the room. Not quite so welcome were the dive bombing birds swooping down on us at meal times pausing only to collect food from the table before exiting on the opposite side. We soon learnt to duck and dive as well as grab hold of our plates as the raids took place. It just added to the experience.

CHIPS WITH EVERYTHING

It didn't take me long to realise that our group naturally divided into two groups, couples and singles. The singles soon formed a friendly alliance. Amongst us was one lady called Daphne, who I think was recovering from an illness. She was good company, mixed in well, and knew about cricket. She also knew a lot about kitchen worktops. We had long conversations about the advantages and disadvantages of granite. This was relevant at the time since, whilst I was enjoying life in the Caribbean, my wife Sue was managing a refit of our kitchen. As I left home the debate on worktops had been settled in favour of granite. Daphne informed me that the downside of granite was that it could chip more easily than you would think, something I can now confirm.

AN EARLY RECCY

Our first full day before the Barbados Test match began was a free day. Some went off on a trip around the island. A few of us went into Bridgetown to have a look around and hopefully visit the cricket ground. The shops were so quaint it was like going back to my childhood as most items were under glass counters or on inaccessible shelves. The deepwater port easily accommodated cruise ships and their passengers were busy shopping in the town.

We headed off to find the cricket ground and were pleased to be able to walk in and have a look round. The Sky television team was out in the middle being shepherded by the floor manager who just happened to be Sarah Botham, daughter of Ian Botham (not yet a Sir as he was Knighted in 2007). We had known for some time that the ticket pricing was going to be unusual. We were charged £360 in total for the ten days of cricket, which was reasonable, compared to prices back home. The unusual element was the decision to charge local people a fraction of this. It soon became clear, however, that we would be in a shady stand, a much better position than the locals who would have to endure that sun for most of the day.

Just outside the ground we found a very welcoming bar selling the famous Red Stripe beer. One thing that stood out was the extremely deep gutters to the side of all the roads but we would see these in action before too long.

HOGGY (MATTHEW HOGGARD) PERFORMS

After boarding the coach for the first day of the Test match at the Kensington Oval, Mike Denness informed us that there would be a sweep based on the score at the close of play. This was to become a regular tradition and on future tours I had the occasional win, but my forecast was a little out this time.

Once at the ground we settled into our seats in the Mitchie Hewitt Stand. It was soon clear that the Brits outnumbered the locals by a huge factor and in that sense, it felt very much a home from home. However, numbers alone were not enough as the atmosphere was very different to that experienced at home. Loud music blasted around the ground and the fantastic aromas emanating from the food stalls set our mouths watering even before the first ball was bowled.

It turned out to be a short but very interesting match with England winning comfortably in just three days, which resulted in us having two extra free days to enjoy the island. England's hero was Hoggy who took a hat- trick (three wickets from consecutive balls) of West Indies wickets. This was the first one I had seen in a Test match, but was certainly not to be the last. We sampled the excellent food with the chicken being particularly good. We also discovered why the gutters in the road were so deep when a cloud burst flooded the pitch and surrounding area. Within minutes of the end of the deluge, however, you wouldn't have known it had rained!

HOGGY PERFORMS OFF THE PITCH TOO

On the first of our unplanned free days we opted for a day of quiet R and R by the pool at the hotel. As we sipped our cold beers looking out to sea we noticed the approach of a rather fine boat. Our attention was alerted by raucous but joyous noise from the vessel. As we watched, a jet ski ridden by two men left the boat and came straight towards us. As it skidded on to the beach the driver remained seated but his passenger wobbled off and staggered towards us. As he got closer we recognised a somewhat worse for wear Hoggy. Apparently, he had come to see his cousin, who was staying at our hotel.

He later told us that Hoggy was being entertained by Lord MacLaurin (former Chairman of the English Cricket Board and Tesco) on his boat and had decided to stop by and say hello. Well it was all Hoggy could do to speak at all. The booze had clearly been flowing aboard that boat. He didn't stay long and was soon seen on the back of the jet ski hurtling to rejoin the celebrations aboard the impressive boat, but not before young James had persuaded Hoggy to have his picture taken with him. Today we would call it a "selfie".

DODGY LOCAL CRICKET

Gullivers had arranged a cricket match against the locals, which we were invited to either watch or take part in. The latter was clearly not an option for me with my poor vision. Colin considered partaking but declared the pitch and outfield "decidedly dodgy" due to an abundance of stones. The locals looked young and athletic, unlike the Gullivers eleven, and this may have had something to do with Colin's decision. We did however boast a young lad who was on the junior books of Northants CCC. Our team also boasted a recently retired professional cricketer, Mark Ilott, a former Essex and England seam bowler who was there fulfilling a similar role to our Mike Denness with another Gullivers group. Mike had not played for a long time and was not about to put his pads back on.

We sat on the benches at the front of the modest wooden pavilion and enjoyed the benefit of a well stocked bar. Mike's partner Doreen made good use of the facility with poor old Mike regularly commanded to refill her empty glass.

The cricket was close with the locals having the edge until our "professional" Mark Ilott took to the crease and launched a series of sixes. I was able to watch the batsman at the crease through my trusted scope but as soon as the shot was struck I could not follow the trajectory of the ball and was forced to rely on the people sat next to me for protection from the incoming fire. This was quite embarrassing as I was regularly found diving for cover when the ball was several feet away, much to everyone's amusement. I remained unscathed and as no one was really concerned about the final score we retreated to a welcome BBQ.

A NIGHT AT THE FORUM

As part of the tour, Gullivers arranged for two of the England players on the fringe of the Test Team to appear at an exclusive 'Gullivers Cricket Forum'. The two players were James Anderson and Rickie Clarke. Aged just 21 and 22 respectively they had made their Test match debuts in the previous year although they had not been selected to play yet in this Test series.

These lads were destined to have very diverse futures. Anderson of course went on to become England's all time leading wicket taker, whereas Clarke did not play in an England Test match again. That night however, they were set to entertain us cricket enthusiasts but due mainly to their age and inexperience they stuck mainly to talking about the current tour.

It was still an interesting event with Rickie Clarke the more confident and entertaining whilst Jimmy Anderson played his quieter, more serious sidekick. The audience were encouraged to ask cricket questions and the players were well chaperoned by a member of the England management team. There were no earthshattering revelations but our young friend James was able to add two more autographs to his collection and enjoyed the bonus of winning a signed cricket bat in the inevitable raffle.

NOT ANOTHER ALAN

Our little "singles" group met regularly throughout the tour particularly for evening meals and drinks. One of the gang was a chap called Alan. Rather unfortunately he reminded me of a lad I went to school with who was also called Alan. Let's call my school "friend" AT. AT and I were acquainted from the time we started Hobmoor Primary School in Birmingham aged five, until AT left Central Grammar in the year we turned sixteen. During those eleven years we never really hit it off. This was strange as we were the only two kids to move from Hobmoor to Central. I don't know why we didn't get on but sometimes you come in to contact with someone where it just doesn't feel right. There were no major falling outs, just a constant lack of friendship. I couldn't get to shake off this feeling of slight unease and I am sure the new Alan must have sensed my reserved approach. I can now say sorry to Alan (but not AT).

Barbados has just about the friendliest locals I have ever had the pleasure to meet. Everyone seemed to wear a constant smile even when chaos reigned at the airport. I also miss the sound of the sea lulling me to sleep. And the cricket wasn't bad either.

"OH WE'RE GOING *FROM* BARBADOS"

The next Test match took us to the island of Antigua just over 300 miles to the north. Barbados airport was less busy than we witnessed on our arrival but still chaotic. This was partly due to the need for everyone to pay a departure tax. A nice little earner with two million passengers paying twenty pounds each, every year.
ANTIGUA

The Caribbean island of Antigua is even smaller than Barbados at just over 100 square miles. Christopher Columbus named it in 1493. The English settlers arrived 150 years later and the connection lasted until 1981. Lord Nelson was a frequent visitor to the island with the dockyards named after him. Notable residents are mostly cricket related and include Sir Viv Richards and Brian Lara. Author Ken Follett also has a home on the island.

A JOLLY TIME

The 300 miles between Barbados and Antigua were covered in not much more than an hour and we soon arrived at the Jolly Beach Hotel. This was very different from the superb Sea Breeze. For a start, it was massive with 5 restaurants and 7 bars, each operating on an all-inclusive basis. There was access to a lovely sandy beach that stretched for a very long way. Surprisingly, there was a full sized cricket pitch and practice nets accessible from the gardens. We were excited to learn that both the England and West Indies cricket teams and umpires were also staying at the Jolly Beach. Although pleasant, my room was much smaller than my previous one and could only really be described as Flintstone-esque. Everything appeared to be fashioned from concrete. Tables, cupboards, chairs everything looked as though it had recently been lifted from Fred Flintstone's cave. Fortunately, the bed had a decent mattress. I shouted for Wilma but no one came.

DIFFERENT PLACE DIFFERENT CULTURE

Margaret, our excellent Gullivers tour manager, had advised us that we would find the locals slightly less friendly than those on Barbados. How right she was! Even on arrival at the airport the staff were lacking in smiles and warmth. We had two free days before the start of the Test match so on the first day Colin and I decided to go into St. John's, the main town. The hotel receptionist had told us that we could get there by taxi for a reasonable set fare. The taxi was called and a large cab duly arrived to pick us up. As we boarded we noticed several other passengers already seated, who shifted to make room for us in the large vehicle. We set off and I confirmed to the driver that Colin and I would be paying one set fare for us both. This was clearly a mistake. Before I knew it, the driver had grabbed my camera and demanded that we must all individually pay the fare. Being a little surprised, I must admit I became a bit cheeky with him. This was a move I soon regretted as he became increasingly aggressive. I quickly resorted to a more apologetic approach and calm was restored along with my camera. We all paid as demanded. Lesson learnt.

St John's town centre was very busy largely due to the arrival of cruise ships and their passengers. The shops near the docking area targeted the ship's tourists, luring them in with gold and other jewellery. We wandered aimlessly for a while until deciding that we weren't that impressed we hailed a taxi to return to the comfort of the familiar Jolly Beach bar. Needless to say, I was on my best behaviour on the journey back, leaving the talking to others. We had been on the island for 24 hours and still hadn't witnessed a smile.

SAFE ON ONE LEG

Somewhat strangely, Admiral Nelson has crept into cricketing terminology. Cricket followers will be aware of the term a "Nelson". This is used when the score reaches exactly 111. It is said that it arose due to Nelson allegedly having only one eye, one arm and one leg. This is of course incorrect, as Nelson never lost a leg, not even over Lady Hamilton. The rumour that the number 111 was therefore unlucky, making a wicket more likely to fall, made umpire David Shepherd raise a leg from the ground when the exact score reached the dreaded number, much to the amusement of many watchers. A study by the 'Cricketer' magazine showed that wickets were no more likely to fall on the Nelson number 111 than any other total. Conclusive proof that, if challenged, whoever came up with this myth wouldn't have a leg to stand on!

BACK ON TWO LEGS

We decided to take a trip out and visited the refurbished dockyards named after Nelson and were immediately impressed. Even allowing for considerable refurbishment they were well worth viewing nearly 200 years after they were built. Nelson lived there for three years from 1784. Whilst there, he met his wife Fanny who was living on the island of Nevis just fifty miles away. They married in 1787 but the marriage fell apart after Nelson began an affair with Lady Hamilton a few years later.

After our visit to the dockyards we headed for the beach where a BBQ awaited. Beach cricket followed for some. It was very enjoyable as I concentrated on the refreshments as usual.

LARA LARA RUNS (Cilla would approve)

As we took our seats on the coach for the first day of the Test at the Recreation Ground, my new friend Colin, had a side bet with Mike Denness that the West Indies prolific batsman Brian Lara would beat the Test record score of 380 set by the Australian Matthew Hayden in the previous year. We all thought Colin was being more than a little optimistic. Colin was soon proven right.

We found our seats in the Andy Roberts Stand. I was delighted to find the presence of television sets attached - somewhat precariously - to the stand supports as this enabled me to clearly see the replays using my scope. It was a very hot day and I drank plenty of water. Colin however, was not so inclined and later regretted this. When he got home his doctor told him that he was suffering the after effects of dehydration, as beer was no substitute for water.

Lara made history again with a record Test score of 400 not out in a West Indies total of 751 for 5 declared. Lara was the

33

first batsman to reclaim the record he had set ten years previously when he had scored 375 on the same ground. He is the only batsman to record Test innings of more than 100, 200, 300 and 400. It was a great achievement and I was delighted to witness it but it was a friendly pitch. We knew from a very early stage the match would inevitably end in a draw and after five days I was suffering a very numb bum!

Our young friend James spent a good deal of the match hunting for autographs. It could almost be described as stalking. He lurked close to the bottom of the steps leading up to the commentary box ready to pounce on unsuspecting cricketing celebrities. We tried to rein in his enthusiasm at times, pointing out that asking players to sign while they were eating at the hotel was 'just not cricket'. He did however capture Lara at one breakfast. You could say he was poached.

After the cricket finished there was very little time left before we were on our way back home. The tour had been everything I had hoped for with the bonus of seeing England win with a Hoggard hat-trick and Lara's world record knock. I needn't have worried about going on my own. Colin and I got on so well we decided that we would like to go on another tour but with me replacing James as his 'roomy' but without the autograph book.

CHAPTER 3 SOUTH AFRICA January 2005

As soon as I got home from the West Indies tour I started researching the next trip. I was delighted to find that England would be touring South Africa in just over six months time. Of the four Tests the team were set to play, I really wanted to go to the third test in Cape Town commencing on the 2nd January. The tours for the previous Tests had been organised for the end of the year but as this tour spanned New Year I was uncertain that I would be able to join part way through.

I contacted Gullivers who informed me that I could fly out on New Year's Day to join the tour in time for the start of the Test. As I was only going for one Test Match this time, I decided to treat myself to the optional additional safari. Having booked the trip, I arranged to have the necessary jabs and stocked up on Malaria tablets.

THE COUNTRY

Cape Town is approximately 6,000 miles from Wetherby and it takes about eleven and a half hours to fly from Heathrow. Having just about uncramped myself from my last long flight, I wasn't relishing the thought of another one. I was pleased to discover, therefore, that the time difference between the UK and South Africa is only a couple of hours so it was less likely that I would suffer with jet lag and I should be able to go straight to the ground on arrival.

South Africa is pretty big, covering over 470,000 square miles, and has a population of over 50 million. Aside from the obvious attractions of the countryside and wild animals, the variety of cultures resulting in no less than eleven official languages, make it a fascinating place.

In 2005 the population were still coming to terms with the adjustments following Mandela's period in office. A change of government and political system had given rise to hope but also some uncertainty.

Some noteworthy facts about South Africa include the distinction of being the only country to build nuclear weapons and then disarm them, being the first country to carry out a heart transplant (conducted in 1967 by Dr Christian Barnard on Lewis Washkansky in Cape Town), and to have two Nobel Peace prize winners living on the same street, Nelson Mandela and Archbishop Desmond Tutu.

Probably due to the huge distances between South African cities, the use of mobile phones is now very high with over 45 million of the 50 million population having mobile phones.

The country has a very successful sporting record particularly in rugby and cricket. It also has more modern day winners of golf majors than any other country, except (of course) the USA.

LESSON ONE

Unlike my previous trip where I had tried to identify fellow travellers by their Gullivers' apparel, this time there was no point looking for other tour party members, as they would have flown before New Year. I felt slightly out of my comfort zone realising that joining the party late would not necessarily be easy. Nevertheless, I boarded the South African Airways flight on the first day of the New Year. Travelling overnight, I managed a few hours sleep despite a very restless neighbour who found it more convenient to rely on me rather than the cabin staff for guidance on operating entertainment and seat controls.

As a lone traveller there was no convenient coach or helpful tour manager waiting for me to arrive, so I headed for the taxi rank to transfer to the very smart Cullinan Waterfront Hotel in Cape Town. Once checked in, I found my room and immediately switched on the television as the match had just started. South Africa had won the toss and were batting first. I decided to dump my bags and join the tour group. Fortunately, my tickets had been left at reception. I quickly boarded a taxi and headed for the Newlands Cricket Ground.

GREAT GROUND BUT COOL RECEPTION

My first impressions of the ground were very positive. It was an attractive combination of modern stands at each end with grassy areas and even the odd tree in between. It was set against a wonderful backdrop of Table Mountain and served excellent Castle beer. You could even see the brewery behind one side of the ground.

By lunchtime the South Africans were two wickets down. I went in search of the Gullivers group, discovering them in a private tent where lunch was being served. I sat next to a couple of chaps who, like me, appeared to be on their own. Despite my friendly banter and engaging demeanour, they were not particularly welcoming for some reason. Due to the overlap with New Year the group was, not surprisingly, largely made up of couples. Even at this early stage of the trip I decided to think carefully before joining future tours late, particularly if I was travelling alone.

Undeterred by the lukewarm welcome, I finished my lunch and settled back in my seat to watch the cricket. The weather was great and the Castle lager stand was all too handy. Jacques Kallis batted well and was 81 not out at close of play, with the total on 247 for 4. South Africa were in a good position.

Back at the hotel I met up with the Gullivers' tour manager, James, in the bar. He was a friendly young lad but unfortunately, he made no attempt to integrate me with my fellow "loners". Looking round the bar, it began to dawn on me why they were loners on a cricket tour with strangers, instead of celebrating the New Year with friends at home. Presumably they hadn't got any, a little harsh perhaps.

On the second day of the Test, Kallis went on to score an impressive 149. He was a fine all rounder who had played for the Old Edwardians in Birmingham as a young lad and was, therefore, known to some friends back in my hometown. At the close, England were faltering at 95 for 4, nearly 350 runs behind. Luckily by this time Keith and Helen, a very nice couple from Berkshire, had befriended me. Like me Keith had also been involved in financial services. He was also very keen on walking and embarked on a campaign to persuade me to join him on a jaunt up Table Mountain. It looked steep and I was not at all keen. I politely made my excuses, so he left it…for now.

The hotel was situated close to the V&A waterfront area by the sea, which offered a good selection of restaurants and bars. It also promised a variety of entertainment. The hotel ran a shuttle bus for the short journey, which proved to be welcome at night when I felt a little more vulnerable. I frequented an excellent sports bar that showed numerous live sports from around the world. It enabled me to watch a bit of live football when I wanted a change from cricket.

By the end of the fourth day the Test was all but over with England 5 wickets down and 349 runs behind. England had been outplayed and South Africa were about to level the series.

TABLE TOPPING

 I finally gave in to Keith's persistence and agreed to "climb every mountain". Well one at least. His clincher was his description of the route we would take. He convinced me that a former prime minister, J. C. Smuts had climbed the route about three times a week until he died at the age of 80. I had no credible excuse and the hike was set for the next day. As it turned out this meant we missed witnessing a rapid and heavy defeat at the cricket.

Being smart, we took the Gullivers coach towards the cricket ground and disembarked at the Botanical Gardens, close to the start of the Table Mountain trail. Unfortunately, we had to pay to enter the gardens even though we only wanted to walk through them to get to the start of the trail. Our plan was to reach the top in time to meet Keith's wife, Helen, at the cable car for lunch.

Keith was a very good guide and as we climbed steadily through the tree line he made sure we stopped regularly to rehydrate and take in the view. It wasn't a varied walk, more like continually climbing up stairs only without the aid of a bannister. In a couple of places ladders were provided to help on particularly steep sections of the climb. Once or twice we had to scramble through scree. At one point we stopped to observe the cricket ground below us in the distance. We couldn't see much action but assumed that an England defeat was inevitable. Indeed it was.

It took well over two hours to reach the 'Table' top but what I hadn't bargained for was the size of the plateau. Although easier walking it took at least another hour for us to stroll across it. We were both glad to see Helen and sit down for a leisurely lunch before our rapid descent by cable car. We caught a public bus back to our hotel, which enabled us to take in interesting parts of the city that we wouldn't usually see. It was a great jaunt, quite an achievement and as I gratefully sank into a warm bath, I was glad that I had been persuaded to go.

PRISON VISITOR

Following England's defeat, we had a couple of free days for sight seeing. I decided that Robben Island was a must. It isn't far off the coast (less than 5 miles) and there are two usual ways of getting there - the slow route and the very slow route. I chose to go on the very slow Susan Kruger Ferry, as this would have been the vessel taken by the prisoners who were transported to the island. It departed from Mandela Gateway at 10.00am and seemed to take forever. The old boat slowly chugged across the waves I wondered about the wisdom of taking the 'authentic' route.

The Robben Island tour lasted about three hours and was very interesting. Our guide was himself an ex-prisoner and presented in a humorous but also poignant manner. Nelson Mandela had spent 18 of his 27 imprisoned years there in a tiny cell. Talk about not being able to swing a cat; he would've struggled to swing a mouse!

A bus trip around the island included a visit to the limestone quarry. This was where Mandela held his "classroom" and spent many hours educating and sharing experiences with fellow inmates in between the interminable rock breaking. At the end of the tour, as there was nothing else to see I chugged my way back to Cape Town's V&A waterfront, thinking about the great man Mandela and his permanent struggle. Was it all going to work out for his country? So far, so good.

The following day I went on the tourist bus tour, which highlighted the great extremes of the city. First, we visited District Six, a working class area that was destroyed under Apartheid laws. The residents were forcibly removed to enable the site to be cleared and developed for white occupation. I don't know where the residents were removed to but despite being empty the area remained untouched for many years. By way of contrast, we were taken to the very smart Campus Bay, an area so affluent that some of the private houses have their own funicular access to the city. Talk about going up the world!

NO LONGER ON MY OWN

As we left Cape Town to follow our non- cricketing options, the size of the party shrank. Only ten of us had opted to take in the mini-safari. We flew north to Tree Lodge, located in the oldest game reserve in Africa. My accommodation was a rustic lodge on legs, with a balcony overlooking a water hole featuring a variety of animals and birds. My new 'room mate' was a persistent gecko who clung to one particular spot on the wall above my bed. He stayed there for virtually the whole of my visit. I couldn't be sure if it was the same one or his twin, as we didn't really have time to get on first name terms. I did try calling him 'El' but didn't get much response.

On the first evening I set off from my lodge towards the central area where dinner was to be served. It was very dark, but about half way along I spotted something on the path. It looked like a branch had been placed across the full width of the path, but as there were no trees nearby this seemed unlikely. Feeling a little unsure, I halted abruptly and then realised that the 'branch' was indeed a large snake. I was reluctant to step over it and equally reluctant to wander off the path into the grassy area, fearing there might be more of his friends lying in wait. After a short time weighing up my options and hoping Mr Snake would quietly slither on his way, I eventually plucked up enough courage to veer off the path and tread very carefully round the obstacle. Once back on the path I virtually ran for the restaurant where the waiter informed me that the snake was most likely harmless. Even so I was grateful that it was not there to greet me on the way back to the lodge. El Gecko was, however, waiting up for me.

The local guides appeared very knowledgeable, so I chose to believe them when they told us that there was no malaria in the region and no need, therefore, to take anti-malarial medication. I'm not sure this was professional advice, but I didn't take the tablets and survived intact. The other thing they insisted on was that if we wanted to see any wildlife we needed to be up and off on our first drive before dawn.

GUNS AT THE READY

We were all up early and left in two large Jeeps, each accompanied by two guides, one of whom had his rifle permanently at the ready. We very soon came across a couple of rhinos in the road; in fact, we almost bumped into them in the half-light. It's apt that the collective noun is a 'crash' of rhinos particularly as they were prevalent in that area.

Well that was one of the 'Big Five' ticked off. We were hoping to spot the others over a series of drives, namely, elephants, lion, leopards, and buffalo. All the guides on the reserve were in radio contact with each other, which helped the drivers locate the best places to find the animals.

The next of the Big Five to be spotted were the elephants. We came across a very unhappy young chap who had become cut off from his herd. The guides thought they had moved south leaving him to fend for himself. He stood in the road blocking our path and before we could get out our cameras, the guides warned us to prepare for a rapid reversal. He began to make loud protests at our arrival and fluids of all descriptions spurted from different parts of his body. Wisely we beat a hasty retreat. There was no doubt that our guides were taking this threat very seriously.

Over the next couple of days, we ventured out on three more drives and managed to see a lion, albeit through binoculars, as he sat unmoving at the top of a distant hill. We also saw buffalo, lots of monkeys and a huge variety of birds but we didn't see a leopard, so we failed in our quest to complete the Big Five.

After several early starts and bumpy mornings spent in the back of a jeep, I treated myself to a relaxing massage, expertly performed in a beautiful setting on my balcony overlooking the water hole. The experience was only slightly spoilt by the masseuse' persistent mention of under payment by the lodge owners. She was clearly hinting for a tip. It was easy to oblige, partly due to the incredible weakness of the Rand.

Two nights, four drives and an encounter with Mr Snake were exciting enough for me. As much as I was going to miss my roommate, I decided against smuggling El home with me. We said our goodbyes and parted on good terms.

Despite not really connecting with any of the Gullivers group, other than Keith and Helen, I had really enjoyed the trip. As I boarded the flight home I was determined to revisit this fascinating country, which I did a few years later and was not disappointed.

CHAPTER 4 INDIA March 2006

Having experienced the disadvantages of going on a tour on my own, I was delighted that my friend Colin who I met on my trip to the West Indies decided to accompany me to India. We were both keen to see the cultural side of this huge country and anticipated that the cricket would be interesting with Andrew Flintoff captaining the side. Colin was excited to fly his 'home town' banner promoting his village of Tinsbury near Bath, which he had flown so successfully in the West Indies.

THE COUNTRY

Stretching just under 2000 miles from north to south and 3000 miles from east to west, India has a coastline of over 4600 miles. This huge country has over 1.2 billion people who make up the largest democracy in the world.

There are lots of interesting things to know about India. Indian housewives, for instance are estimated to hold at least 11% of the world's gold, which is more than the gold reserves of the USA, Germany and Switzerland added together. This does not even include the country's own gold reserves. It was also the first country to mine diamonds.

It has the world's largest film industry based in Mumbai. It also claims to have invented both Chess and Snakes and Ladders. Perhaps its greatest sporting claim to fame is being home to the highest cricket ground in the world at Chail, built in 1893 and standing some 2444 metres above sea level.

WRONG SEAT

The first half of our trip was to be spent sightseeing. Starting in Delhi before moving to visit the area known as the Golden Triangle, which includes Agra and Jaipur. We would then move down to Mumbai to enjoy the Test Match. Our flight from London to Delhi was 4100 miles long and would take just over eight hours.

I had decided that as the first flight was during the day I did not need to go to the expense of business class. I opted instead for the extra leg room that premium economy provided, saving the business class luxury for the return journey from Mumbai.

All was going well on the outward flight until I noticed that the chap sitting next to me was not at all well. He sweated profusely and did not rise from his seat during the entire flight. Travelling by air is hazardous as the air is recirculated and those nasty germs along with it. There is little defence from someone sitting and breathing right next to you for over 8 hours, as I would soon find out.

THEY "SIKH" HIM HERE

Despite my concerns regarding the recirculated air on the flight, I woke up on the first day in our smart New Delhi hotel feeling pretty good. We boarded our coach for a tour of the capital. Our local guide was pure entertainment as he took us from one sight to another. He was a Sikh wearing a traditional turban. Sikhs make up less than 2% of the population of India, in contrast to Hindus who account for about 80%, and Muslims at around 15%.

My main memory of our coach tour was the huge difference between New and Old Delhi. New Delhi has wide streets and is home to the embassies of the main nations, whereas Old Delhi is seemingly just a mass of people. The shops in Old Delhi were incredible. The butchers were out on the pavement with their produce open to the elements for all to see (and possibly handle!). Electrical joints and wires hung precariously from buildings, looking as though they would either fall to the ground or spontaneously combust at any moment. There were a large number of shops exclusively selling used cardboard. This was initially baffling until we were informed that sadly, this was for the many homeless people to cover themselves at night.

As the day wore on my initial 'joie de vivre' wore off. In fact I started to feel so tired and disorientated that I left the evening meal with our new tour colleagues early in search of my bed. Colin and I were sharing a very smart twin room with the most enormous flat screen TV. The hotel in general and our room in particular was of an extremely high standard supported by superb staff. This was fortunate as I rapidly realised that I was not well and would be requiring assistance from said staff. It is a great pity that I cannot recall the name of the hotel.

MISSING OUT

I had a very restless night and subsequently the next morning I could not get out of bed. Colin and the rest of the party were heading off to visit the Golden Triangle. As much as I had been looking forward to this part of the tour, it was apparent that I really needed to stay put. Colin helpfully summoned the tour manager, John, before saying cheerio for a few days.

John and I decided the hotel doctor should be called. My symptoms were a severe sore throat, persistent headache and high temperature. I was pretty sure I was suffering from a nasty bout of tonsillitis. The doctor turned up and took my blood pressure, which, partly because of 'white coat syndrome', was quite high. He instantly declared that I must go to the cardiac unit for my heart to be thoroughly checked. Although struggling to talk I politely refused, pointing out that I was suffering from a sore throat not imminent cardiac arrest. I instructed him to leave and not to return.

Fortunately, before the Gullivers tour manager headed off to the Golden Triangle, he agreed to leave me in the 'capable' hands of their local agent Mr. Rao. This turned out to be very interesting.

The local agent, Mr. Rao appeared and informed me that 'everything was under control' and that he had arranged for me to go to the home of a consultant to be examined. Even in my poorly state I was unaware that 'everything had been *out* of control' or that I needed consultant care. Probably paracetamol and throat lozenges would suffice. Nevertheless, he returned a couple of hours later and I was placed in a wheelchair and carefully pushed through the hotel lobby to his waiting car.

His driver helped install me on the back seat and we set off. What I didn't realise was that this was a special day, the Festival of Colours, or Holi Festival. Delhi was heaving! Most of the 14 million residents were out on the streets throwing coloured powder everywhere. It was mayhem. I was glad to be seated in the rear of the car as the driver patiently threaded his way through the crowds.

The doctor was pleasant and seemed very capable. After a brief examination he pronounced, somewhat reassuringly, that I did indeed have tonsillitis not heart failure. I had suffered the condition many times as a child but only once as an adult some years earlier and not as severely as this. He wrote me a prescription and informed Mr Rao that because of the festival we would need to get the medication from the hospital. He also gave me the good news that I should be fit to travel down to Mumbai for the Test later in the week.

DRUG RUNNING

I was helped back to the car and once again the agent, driver and I threaded our way through the festival chaos to the hospital. The journey wasn't too bad until we reached the track into the hospital itself. Again, there were people and cars everywhere but nothing was moving into the grounds. I started to grow impatient and longed for the comfort of my bed when suddenly the car lurched forward. I looked up to discover that we were heading the wrong way down the hospital exit road. Once or twice the driver was forced to swerve to avoid oncoming traffic but he appeared confident. I was terrified but thankfully we were soon close enough to stop and allow Mr Rao to leave the car and go drug running. My head hurt a lot so I was extremely glad to eventually get back to my bed and the cool and calm of my room.

Despite feeling exhausted, I switched on the oversized TV. This was a mistake! A game show was playing and as I drifted in and out of sleep I started to hallucinate. Before long I was taking part in the show, or at least I thought I was. The good news was that I WON! I can't remember what I won but it was probably a fondue set.

My health gradually improved over the next couple of days, helped by the excellent care of the hotel staff. They brought me fresh flowers every day and tempting morsels of food as my appetite returned. I particularly remember a young lad in uniform who was sent out to buy me Strepsils and other remedies each day. He was great, and clearly overwhelmed by the small gratuity offered to him each visit.

BOMBAY WITHOUT DUCKS

By the time the rest of the group returned to the hotel with stories of their wonderful time visiting stunning places such as the Taj Mahal and the Amber Fort. I was almost back to full strength. Determined not to miss out again I declared myself well enough to fly to Mumbai. I think I preferred the city's old name, Bombay.

We arrived during the early evening before the Test commenced. This left no time to look round but we enjoyed a good night in the hotel whose name I have failed to recall. It was set in beautiful grounds with opulent décor, a really outstanding hotel, up there with the best I have had the good fortune to visit anywhere in the world. The contrast seen throughout India was just as evident. Immediately outside the walled and manicured gardens, the pavements were full of people settling amongst the cardboard to sleep for the night, but amazingly an air of acceptance was ever present. Back in our cosseted world we had discovered a very "happy hour" where the drinks were free. Colin and I were a little peeved that it took us almost the whole of the "happy hour" to discover this delight but we made full use of it over the next few days making it a happy week.

TIGHTLY GUARDED STADIUM

The journey to the unfortunately titled Wankhede Cricket Stadium took about half an hour. We drove through the busy streets passing the railway station on the way. As a train slowly rattled its way out of the station, I was fascinated to see people hanging off the roof and out of the windows. There were bodies everywhere. I had seen similar sights on TV, but this was everyday life in India. Mumbai was more like Old Delhi, with masses of people but with the addition of the Indian Ocean.

By now, I had started to consider myself an international and dare I say it, experienced cricket fan. I had my usual supplies to take into the ground. First, and most important was my scope, without which I would see very little. The next essential was sun cream, closely followed by water. When available, an English newspaper would also be included and this time it was as India has regular papers in English. Finally, I would have a sun hat, either in the Gullivers bag or on my head.

We stood in line waiting for the usual security check but were amazed to have not only our water removed but also our newspapers. The explanation given for confiscation of newspapers was that we could set fire to them. Of course, we wouldn't, not even if Piers Morgan was found grinning at us from the front page.

The reason for the water removal was a little more complicated. One explanation was that the bottle might contain gin or vodka that clearly looks very similar to water but usually tastes a whole lot different. However, that didn't seem to be an adequate explanation. Like me, Colin enjoyed a drink but I was confident his bottle was also Adam's ale.

On entering the ground several rather disconcerting facts became apparent. The place was filthy, as it had clearly not been cleaned for months. The dust and dirt was so deep it was ready for planting and would have supported a fair crop. Our tickets provided seat numbers but we were soon informed that they were usually ignored. As we were early, John, our tour manager, took the opportunity to shepherd us into an area that was, thankfully, in the shade.

We sat down and within moments a group of young boys appeared with trays of foil covered plastic cups containing water. Aha! Mystery solved. Well partly, as almost at that exact moment, a large notice appeared on the giant screen accompanied by a Tannoy message informing us that we were not to buy the water from the small boys as they were 'unofficial' and 'over charging'. The pricing accusation was hard to swallow as you could buy a whole tray for next to nothing so Colin and I and most of the crowd, ignored the request and supported the boys rather than buy the official product. This was an example of young entrepreneurs in action, rather than child labour.

INDIAN TAKEAWAY

At the start of the match, England were one down in the three match series and had not won a Test match on Indian soil for 21 years. Our hopes of witnessing a rare victory were not high but things started well with England opener Strauss compiling a rather understated 128 and debutant Owais Shah striking 88, leaving the side on 272 for the loss of 3 wickets at close of play on the first day.

Three more good days followed for England, which left India needing 300 to win on the last day with 9 wickets left standing. They were 75 for 3 at lunch but collapsed to 100 all out losing by 212 runs, enabling England to square the series. England captain Flintoff steamed in to take 3 wickets and pick up the Man of the Series award. Spin bowler Udal took 4 wickets at the age of 37 in his last Test. The local crowd stood and applauded England and many of them shook our hands and thanked us for coming to their country. Amazing people! Great event!

Back at our hotel we took full advantage of the free bar, after which we were invited to a special event on the top floor with food and more free drinks. Among the guests was the comedian and presenter Nick Hancock, but he didn't do a turn as he too was there for the cricket.

The following day Gullivers organised a cricket forum at a local cricket club out near the Test ground. Guest speakers included the former Lancashire players, Jack Bond and Jack Simmonds. All good stuff for cricket lovers, particularly those from Lancashire. On the down side, Colin and I were disappointed to find that for a change we had to pay for our drinks. It was, however, a fitting finale to an eventful tour.

I found India to be a fascinating country with wonderful people, so accepting of their lot. It also has some of the best hotels I have had the good fortune to stay in. My only real regret was missing out on some of the magical sights during the first week including, of course, the Taj Mahal. Colin was great company and as a result, I decided that I would always try to have a friend with me on any future tours.

GOOD NEWS MR DUFFIN

The flight back home took slightly longer than the journey to Delhi and was preceded by a pleasant surprise at the check-in desk. As I handed over my details the clerk said that business class was over booked and they were looking for volunteers to move back to premium economy. There was a substantial cash incentive plus full refund of the difference in cost. As the flight time was again in daylight, I decided to take the offer and went off to relax (and stretch out) in the business class lounge whilst awaiting boarding.

When I eventually proceeded towards the departure gate, I was taken to one side and informed that there had been another change. I was now being upgraded to first class. My reaction was one of disappointment as I had mentally adjusted to the situation and in my head, I had already spent the cash. Hard to believe that I had been upgraded to first class at no cost and was still disappointed. Poor me!

CHAPTER 5 AUSTRALIA November 2006

I could not resist the opportunity to follow an Ashes tour in Australia. My friend and fellow Yorkshire member Stuart Rhodes decided to join me for the two Tests in Brisbane and Adelaide. Another first was my decision to take my laptop and send home blogs to friends and family.

SEPARATED AT "BERTH"

Being an 'old hand' at cricket tours I assured Stuart I would take the lead with booking. From my first contact with Kuoni Sport Abroad, however, I had a feeling things were not going to be as straightforward as I hoped. Simple questions such as "Do you have any spaces on the Outback tour?" were disconcertedly greeted with "Can you call back when Colin is here?"

My Kuoni confidence was further tested over the next few weeks as I received a stream of 'revised' invoices even though no booking details had changed. To top it all, on the Friday before our Sunday departure a chance remark (after another bottle of Beaujolais Nouveau) uncovered the fact that Stuart and I were travelling on different airplanes. This was news to both of us! It was too late to change our plans and we settled back for another glass of wine hoping for the best.

FLYING BACKWARDS FOR CHRISTMAS (apologies to fans of the Goons)

One of the benefits of flying these days is being able to log onto the website and choose your seats. Well that is the theory, but when I tried, all the pre-booked seats had already been allocated. Being a persistent sort of chap, I kept trying and had some success. Logging on to the site 24hrs before flying I discovered that my seat (E16) had already been allocated, couldn't be changed and that was that. Feeling indignant I checked to see where exactly I had been put only to discover that seat E16 faced backwards! I sat and contemplated the wisdom of flying half way around the world at 500 miles per hour facing the way I had just come.

Despite travelling on different planes, Stuart and I were travelling from the same airport at roughly the same time. We considered it a small victory that, pre-boarding, Stuart and I 'wangled' our way into the BA lounge, despite the protestations of Miss BA sourpuss 2006. After a swift G&T, my flight was announced and I left Stuart in the lounge. On boarding BA15 bound for Sydney, I found my backwards facing seat and having not really come to terms with the weirdness of this, I looked enviously at fellow passengers settling into their forward facing seats. It was then that I spotted a potential opportunity to move, to a seat at least facing the right way and possibly one positioned up where the big boys play, by the driver. I hatched my plan and requested a glass of water from the eager attendant. Seemingly unintentionally, I swiftly knocked the glass spilling water all over my seat. In my view this rendered it completely useless and I rapidly sought the attendant's attention to request a move.

Unfortunately, the flight attendant had spotted the incident and rushed up with a standard issue BA rug to cover the seat and consequently declared it fully operable. Accepting failure, I slumped into the now damp E16 and prepared for reverse take off.

Although long, the rest of the flight was uneventful and I even came to accept that it is actually impossible to tell which way you are travelling provided, of course, you don't look out the window and also ignore take-off and landing. I did, however see two dawns on the Monday, neither of which was spelt with a capital D!

SHOWERS IN SYDNEY

We had a brief stop to change planes in Sydney and I took a very welcome opportunity to refresh by having a shower, courtesy of Qantas before boarding the next plane. A quick hop up to Brisbane meant that I was quickly reunited with Stuart at the very pleasant Conrad Treasury Hotel, shortly after 10:00am local time. Our simple task for the day was to stay awake for the next 12 hours to try to fool our bodies into thinking they had adjusted to Brisbane time.

We managed the first few hours quite well. We strolled without a care on the picturesque south bank of the Brisbane River until lunchtime. Settling at our table at "Timmy's", we congratulated ourselves for successfully overcoming jetlag but this complacency led to a foolish error.

We sampled the local white wine and fatigue spread through our bodies in almost perfect synchronicity with the alcohol. We tried more walking but this made us even wearier so we decided to give ourselves a break by boarding the 'Citycat', a commendable riverboat service. We stood in the sun, we stood out of the sun, we tried standing face into the breeze, but the weariness persisted and once we sat down our heads began to droop. We rapidly went through the whole 'standing in and out of the sun/breeze' routine. In fact, we tried everything short of singing, as we were sure the locals would not appreciate this.

Eventually we decided the best form of defence was attack, and disembarking at the riverbank we found the nearest pub. Not the wisest decision. By 9.00pm we didn't give a 'FourX' about anything as we were tucked up back at the Conrad Treasury fast asleep.

Not surprisingly, we were awake ridiculously early the next morning and set off in search of a Brisbane breakfast. In a nearby café we rapidly demolished a "Coffee Club" breakfast and felt set up to discover Brisbane.

After a long meandering walk we came across the Nautical Museum and decided to go in. We approached the ticket office where, upsettingly, we were offered two senior discounts! I must point out that Stuart was in front of me and I was wearing both a hat and sunglasses. The curator's quip about not checking birth certificates did not help. The museum was not particularly interesting it did not float my boat (apologies) but at least we had not paid the full price.

At this point I feel I must mention that Stuart decided he was hungry again so we set off for the café where he had his second 'full English' of the day. We strolled the banks of the river and began to get our Brisbane bearings.

In the evening we meet up with the rest of the tour group to attend a courtesy barbeque. We were entertained by a couple of former Australian Test cricketers, namely Carl Rackermann and Rodney Hogg. They were pretty good speakers and it turned out to be an amusing evening despite the relentless "pommie bashing". We didn't really click with any other members of the tour at this point, as chaps on their own seemed to be in short supply.

DOWN TO BUSINESS

The cricket started. That is to say the Australians started, we didn't. Our opening bowler, Harmison, bowled the widest first ball in Ashes history (straight to second slip) and our unsuccessful struggle to assert ourselves began. To add insult to injury, after play ended our coach was so late we were still at the ground almost an hour after stumps were drawn, leaving us to wallow in a collective state of depression.

By coincidence or design, an excellent function that evening helped to take our minds off the first day's battering. Derek Pringle (former England pace bowler) was part of a panel fielding questions. He announced that the team was under prepared and needed Monty (Panasar - spin bowler). Not sure if he was thinking of the cricketer or the Flying Circus.

MORE OF THE SAME

Day Two and we were really getting stuffed. It was painful to watch. One woman in our group was so enthralled by the play that after an hour she took out a colouring book and a packet of crayons (seriously). Security was way over the top for no apparent reason, even the Barmy army bugler had been ejected. The Mexican wave was also banned. Probably as a reaction to this, a game of 'pass the beach ball' started, which was rapidly curtailed by officious stewards grabbing the offending articles and putting them to the sword.

On the pitch, only Flintoff emerged with any real pride although Hoggy (Matthew Hoggard) did put in a much better spell after lunch. The modern stadium provided good facilities and perfect viewing, but the lack of any character, together with splitting up the England fans did nothing for the atmosphere.

STRAIGHT BAT

Away from the cricket, Stuart and I had a decent meal and a good bottle of wine which we sipped overlooking the Story Bridge which looks a bit like the Sydney Bridge only smaller.

This went some way to easing our discomfort at being England fans. On the way back to our hotel we experienced an extraordinary and somewhat frightening moment when a swarm of very large fruit bats which had been innocuously perching in the trees suddenly decided to take flight and headed straight towards us. Instinctively we ducked rapidly, and then stood to admire the sight of so many of the creatures before making our way back to our hotel.

BILLY BOWS DOWN

England's batting collapse on a good pitch (bar the odd crack) was painful to watch. Only Bell emerged with any real credit. The Aussie decision to bat again sent us all searching for our colouring books. Only the sight of umpire Billy Bowden being almost cut in two with a vicious pull shot provided any enjoyment. It was a memorably disappointing day for English cricket.

By way of entertainment for the day, Stuart and I had taken to observing (and nicknaming) the fans around us. We noticed one guy sitting further along our row who had developed a strange pattern of going back and forth all day. We dubbed him 'Yoyo Man'. We stood up countless times to let him out, then five minutes later we were up to let him back in again. A weak bladder could not be the cause as the intense heat meant that an average bladder would only yell for help once every few hours even after drinking serious volumes of fluids. The mystery surrounding 'Yoyo man 'continued unresolved.

The Aussie second innings was so meaningless that the local game of beach ball tossing started up again, but this time with a twist. From nowhere a blow-up doll emerged and was being tossed all around the stands creating an interesting diversion. Immediately attention moved from the cricket to the inflatable.

Predictably, the stewards made their move, but this merely increased the crowd's determination to avoid capture of the fair maiden. After much sport she was apprehended, but the amusement was not over as a young officer struggled to hold the offender in a dignified manner. Suffice it to say all eyes watched intently to see if the maiden would go down on him. We were disappointed by lack of cricket action but overall delighted that 'pass the inflatable' had taken on a new dimension.

DAY FOUR AND THE BOYS ARE BACK (WELL SORT OF)

A spirited display of determined batting from Collingwood and Pietersen brought the English supporters back to life. Cook showed some composure and Bell seemed a touch unlucky. Only a few injudicious strokes from Strauss and Flintoff and the dismissal of Collingwood could be criticised. There was much to cheer and the Aussie attack looked far from invincible. Talk of storm clouds spread rapidly amongst the Barmy Army, but my head told me it was an impossible task and my heart could do little else but agree.

THEY THINK IT'S ALL OVER...............

On the final day we arrived at the ground under a cloudy sky. Could the great escape be on? First of all, we had to wait for the power to be restored as a power cut had disabled the ticket scanners. As we took our seats our hopes of escape were soon dashed. The end came abruptly as the clouds vanished almost as quickly as the last five English batsmen. We had no alternative but to walk from the ground to the delightful South Bank and grab a cold one by way of consolation. At least the Barmy Army were able to congregate and sing (rather optimistically) after losing the first of a five Test series, "we're going to win four one".

Back at the hotel we packed for our trip to Ayers Rock, or as some locals call it "that bl***y big red thing".

WHAT ARE THE ODDS?

Have you ever looked at coincidences and tried to calculate the odds of the event happening? Now I am not against people being overweight but we had a guy on our tour who was a very large chap. On arriving at my seat at the Gabba (the Brisbane cricket ground) it was apparent that I was to spend the next five days wrestling with the big man.

There were about sixty people in our group so the odds of sitting one side of our friend were thirty to one. Now the next allocation of seats was for our flight to Ayers Rock via Sydney. It was the same size of party so there were similar odds of being seated with the big man. Well I pulled a double. Shame there was no book as I was now up at 900 to 1. He disembarked for a couple of days in Sydney so all further bets were off. He was the real winner, however, as he had swapped a trip to the big red thing for a couple of days in lovely Sydney.

THAT BIG RED THING

How daft is daylight saving time (DST) in Oz? Not all states are compliant which makes keeping track of time very tricky. We left Brisbane at 6.30am where there is no DST, and arrived in Sydney at 8.00am, where they do have DST. In accordance our watches were duly moved on to 9.00am. But as we boarded our flight for Ayers Rock, which was due to land at 1.30pm, we were told to put our watches back one and a half hours to midday. Flying in the same direction we had put clocks both forward and back! Confused? We were!

Now when they say it is hot in the middle of the country, they mean hot. Well over 40c during the day. Sensibly we were advised not to venture out between 10.00am and 4.00pm – quite a chunk of the day - and if we were tempted to explore we would need to drink at least a litre of water every hour to stay hydrated. What were we going to do for the next 36 hours? Clearly lots of fun to be had here then!

We set out for the sunset viewing of 'The Rock' just after 6.00pm, approximately one hour before the main event. We were issued with our tickets to the park and told repeatedly that we must have them with us at all times whilst in the park. As we passed through the park barrier we were told to hold our precious tickets in our right hand and wave them furiously whenever instructed. We all knew it was daft but did it anyway, probably because we were Brits.

It's worth reminding ourselves that we had flown for five hours on two planes to be there, not to mention the mind warping 'time travel'. It's also worth noting that in order to witness the true spectacle of Ayers Rock at sunset you only need two things: the big red thing and the sun. One out of two is really not enough. The champagne was welcome and the nibbles took the edge of our hunger. As for the big red rock, it was still there.

Sensing some disappointment our guide reassured us that we wouldn't have to wait long for our next chance to be captivated. As we arrived back at the Sails in the Desert Hotel we were told to be outside at 04.50 ready to board the coach to witness the spectacle of sunrise at the big red rock.

You're ahead of me; there was no rise and no sun. The sky grew lighter but the clouds were still there to spoil the party. Now you know how often we were told to have our tickets with us on pain of death? Well Stuart somehow managed to forget this instruction and embarrassingly was sent back to his room by the driver. Clearly time was of the essence and he had to run. He was so out of breath on his return that I started to look round for potential 'kiss of death' volunteers.

Thankfully resuscitation was not necessary and the now recovered Stuart took the best photos that the clouds would allow. We then did a couple of short walks up at the rock and saw a few rock paintings. Overall the rock was underwhelming and left me thinking that a couple of days in Sydney would have been far more rewarding.

For those of you who, like me, have wondered how the big red rock got to be there, well in a sentence, it was laid down under the sea as a huge sinkhole, collected sediment and was later tilted by plate movement, followed by retreating of the sea. Feel better for that? I know I do.

On returning to the hotel, the heat was incredible, and we didn't venture out until hunger took over. However, we saw one being who had no problem with the conditions: we watched, a little warily as a huge lizard slowly made his way between the hotel buildings. We didn't disturb him as this was clearly his territory.

As this was our last night in the desert, we made a careful trek to the Outback Pioneer hotel via a short cut across some decidedly dodgy terrain. Saving just five minutes in the heat was worth the risk of meeting some of Australia's more dangerous inhabitants.

The Outback restaurant advertised an interesting menu, offering many types of Australian tucker from kangaroo to emu. We tried several without any serious repercussions. The return trek to our hotel after nightfall was along the safety of what passed for a pavement. It was a reasonable end to an uninspiring trip to Ayers Rock or to give it the correct name, Uluru.

WELCOME TO ADELAIDE

We arrived at the Hilton Adelaide at just after 8.00pm and received an immediate instruction to report to the Balcony Room for drinks with Australian cricket celebrities Rodney Hogg (again) and Terry Jenner (former spinner and Shane Warne's coach). TJ was excellent, both informative and entertaining. He gave us his view on Yorkshire's young leg spinner, Adil Rashid, as he had already worked with him. Stuart and I had seen Rashid make his debut earlier in the summer at Scarborough, taking six wickets in the second innings at the age of eighteen. TJ said he thought he could be a Test player but must be careful not to be distracted by spending too much time working on his batting. Wise words indeed. Hogg had been OK in Brisbane, but he was not so hot here as he resorted to over indulging in pommie bashing.

It was more than a little strange to find ourselves surrounded by the trappings of a traditional Christmas with the sun beating down sending us searching for shade.

The Adelaide Hilton looks out over Victoria Square or 'Tarndanyangga' - loosely translated as 'the dreaming place of the red kangaroo'. It was also the resting place of a giant, highly decorated Christmas tree whose lights competed feebly against the sun. Inside the hotel reception, a model train chugged and whistled, endlessly circulating through snow covered scenery. It was all very festive but it didn't feel quite right.

GREAT CRICKET AND A BIT OF LUCK

The first day of the 2nd Test at the Adelaide Oval was a great cricket day. After a cautious start, the England boys gradually increased the batting pace to end the day at over 250 with the loss of only three wickets. In stark contrast to the previous days of sweltering heat, however, we sat and shivered. Boy it was cold! Yes cold. In fact, when the south wind blew (like the north wind for us Brits when at home) it was freezing. It was so cold in our temporary seating (Chappell stand) that the coffee queue was three times longer than the queue for beer.

We were up very early on the second day for Terry Jenner's "Test Brekkie". By 7.30am, over 900 people sat waiting in anticipation of food and entertainment. Guests such as cricketers Shane Warne and Glen McGrath plus other local speakers put on a pretty good show talking about the Test match plus a few anecdotes.

There was the usual auction and inevitable raffle. The first prize in the raffle was a smart plaque recording Sir Donald Bradman's career and signed by the great man himself. It was a slightly different kind of raffle as receiving a playing card automatically entered us. I was dealt a joker that meant I got trough the first round before further luck saw me continue to advance. The odds of winning were pretty slim, in fact almost identical to being seated next to 'the big man' on successive occasions as had happened previously. This time, despite the odds, I was delighted to be on the winning end and collected the plaque with a sense of karma being restored. Placing a treble on all three events would have given the bookies a shock.

FLAT OUT FOR BREAKFAST

On subsequent mornings in Adelaide, we fell into a different breakfast routine. Rather than pay the high price of the Hilton breakfast, we found a very convenient cafe just around the corner inside the entrance to the indoor market. This served an appetizing full Australian breakfast, and I discovered the joy of 'flat white' coffees, which were yet to make an impression on the UK.

Back at the cricket, England's batting went from strength to strength as Collingwood hit 200 and KP (Kevin Pietersen) smacked 158. At 551 for six, Captain Flintoff declared, placing us in a very strong position going forward.

STALKED BY A BACKPACK

I must mention the extreme efficiency of the Conrad Treasury Hotel back in Brisbane. When I returned to my hotel room at the end of the first day's play in Adelaide, I was surprised to find a huge parcel waiting for me. My excitement increased as I tore open the neat packaging, and was replaced by incredulity when I looked inside to find an item I didn't even know I had 'lost'.

The Kuoni Tour Company had given us all complementary backpacks, seat cushions and sun hats. However, the Gabba cricket ground's security people in Brisbane had decided to ban backpacks so I decided I didn't want it and left mine behind in the hotel room. The seat cushions proved to be as much use as a chocolate fireguard and the expensive Gray-Nicholls hats were too small for almost everyone. Most of us had tried offloading our hats onto the group hobbit (who shall remain nameless) and although initially delighted, he rapidly became saturated with unwanted hats.

The aforesaid items were deliberately left in or around the waste paper bin in our hotel room. Stuart loves to read and he had devoured three paperbacks. These were added to the pile before we left. Amazingly backpacks, books, hats and cushions had all escaped the expected disposal, had followed us 1000 miles across Australia and were now to be found in room 415 of the Adelaide Hilton. This was undoubtedly fantastic service from the Brisbane hotel staff, but we still didn't want the useless freebies. Determined to dispose of the unwanted goods this time we left a note for our cleaner making it very clear that the stalking was not to be repeated.

A DRAW LOOKS VERY LIKELY

Meanwhile back at the cricket, the freezing cold wind meant that my fleece stayed firmly fastened until the sun came around at about 3.00pm. A couple of Australian wickets in the first session led to a brief rise in our level of optimism. A wicketless session after lunch put paid to that. A draw was now almost certain as the Aussies passed 500. 'Yoyo man' was back sitting on our row and up to his old 'up down, up down' tricks. He was back and forth too many times to count. Being optimistic, we agreed that he was helping the whole row keep DVT at bay! The reason for his jaunts remained a mystery.

That evening, Stuart and I attended another cricket dinner. Former England captain Graham Gooch and current Aussie selector and former fast bowler Mervyn Hughes were in full flow. 'Merv" summed up their thoughts on the current match by declaring that a draw was a 'certainty'.

THE BOYS PLAY TRUANT

The previous days' cricket had been interesting and entertaining but the last couple of sessions, along with Merv's comments, convinced us that a draw was on the cards. Accepting this inevitability convinced us to play hooky and have a look around Adelaide instead. The tram to the beach at Glenelg stopped just outside our hotel. In a little over twenty minutes we were disembarking at the seaside. The chilly wind had gone and it was a 'beaut'! We enjoyed our time with a relaxed coffee and read of Aston Villa's 2-2 thriller at 'Pompey'. Yet another draw, but this time a distinct improvement on the recent stuffing at Man City.

We took the tram into town and then strolled through the botanical gardens. We paid some attention to the flora whilst really focusing on finding the shortest route to the wine tasting at the South Australia Wine Experience. We tried as many wines as we were allowed, to accompany our lunch. A very pleasant experience.

Close by was the Sir Donald Bradman collection and the Ashes attraction. The Don collection was interesting, but I find it hard to understand all the fuss about the little urn. The one with the short fat hairy legs was much better.

On our way back to the Hilton we took a detour via the shops to buy something to protect my valued raffle prize. The Don's signature, written in felt tip on top of clear plastic covering the plaque appeared to be more than a little vulnerable. So vulnerable ten years later it has completely disappeared. The shop assistant looked a bit bemused when I presented Blue-tac, a set of paper plates, a plastic folder plus a roll of Sellotape. I felt obliged to explain that I was not setting up a Blue Peter "Tracey Island", but trying to protect a precious item in transit.

LUCKY TO COME SECOND

We had a memorable last day at the Adelaide Oval. I realise that looking forward to a draw is a bit sad, but in truth, we were. At the end of play on the fourth day the omens were good. England's batsmen Strauss and Bell were looking solid and my unlucky shirt had been confined to the wash basket. What could go wrong?

Well, just about everything. For a start the seats in which we had previously been shivering were now red hot. The wind had completely changed direction from the cold Antarctic southwest to the desert dry north. Gone were the fleece and hot coffee, it was now cold beer and shade in high demand as the long queues testified.

As for the cricket, the usually reliable umpire Steve Bucknor incorrectly gave out Strauss. Then Bell dropped another clanger. KP swept for the first time against Warne and the slide towards defeat commenced. The tension rose as overs became as important as runs. Flintoff appeared to let the weight of captaincy rest heavily on his bat. Jones slashed at a ball that may have been called a wide if he had not stretched out so far. The tail tried to hang around with every ball cheered and every run scored prompting an ovation from the Barmy Army and the rest of us Poms. Giles failed to protect anything except his body and a certain 'put your house on a draw' (Merv Hughes) had been handed to the Aussies. They say that sport at the highest level is won and lost in the head. That day we looked and played like headless chickens. It is not often that a Test team loses after scoring over 500 runs and declaring with plenty of wickets still standing. Embarrassingly we managed it.

Still, it's only a game and we had important things to ponder like which restaurant we should choose. We selected a Thai, and things looked a whole lot better.

INTO THE BAROSSA VALLEY

We had one free day left and booked a trip to the Barossa Valley with the promise of great scenery, a delicious lunch and two wine tasting sessions. It was very pleasant and fairly uneventful, except for the chap sitting in front of us on the coach. He started to feel a little uncomfortable, as the giant coach swung more than any English bowler had managed as it snaked along the winding roads. The poor chap was clearly struggling and eventually staggered to the loo sited (unfortunately) near our seats. I knew he was in trouble when he closed the door and the vacant sign remained. Previous experience (as my daughter Claire will remember in America) has taught me that the cabin light only comes on when the door is locked. He was in trouble.

The door came half open twice as we swerved round the bends. In the confusion his nausea got the better of him. Later the poor chap was full of apologies to the driver as he tried to explain how he had emptied the contents of his stomach in the dark with inevitable lack of accuracy.

We whizzed through our first wine tasting so fast that it felt as though some sort of record was being attempted. We managed to briefly taste a startling eight wines in twenty five minutes, including a sparkling wine, a port and a substantial piece of chocolate to accompany the £50 red. They were only sips but Roy Castle would have been turning in his grave!

Even more remarkable was that the coach "chucker" was first in the line, amazingly holding it all in.

All in all, it was a very enjoyable tour. The cricket had its moments, despite England's performance. It was great to see more of Australia and even the visit to Ayers Rock will stay in my memory for many years. It was a pity the group didn't really gel. This was partly due to its size and the inability of the tour manager to integrate the people effectively. Our next tour would be far more successful in this respect.

CHAPTER 6 NEW ZEALAND March 2008

Although Stuart, my cricket buddy, and I enjoyed our trip to Australia we were both a little disappointed by the tour company. There were too many on the tour which, combined with the lacklustre tour manager, resulted in very little group bonding. We decided to try a different operator for our next trip. After a good look at the contenders we decided to go with the (aptly named) Cricket Tour Company. We were impressed by their stated commitment to provide a high quality tour without losing the personal touch. They appeared to be offering a tour that was much more than just cricket.

THE COUNTRY

It is common knowledge that New Zealand consists of two main islands Despite being a small country it offers spectacular and varied scenery ranging from volcanoes to glaciers. Perhaps less well known is that wherever you are in the country, you will never be more than about 80 miles from the sea. Even less appreciated is that there are roughly 50 million possums running around the islands. They massively outnumber the sheep, numbers of which have steadily declined to around 30 million from a high of 70 million in the early 1980s due to a switch to dairy farming.

The human population is c4.5 million with about 85% of European descent. The Maori population is c700,000. All this adds up to a fascinating country with beautiful scenery, relatively few people, and many, many unwanted furry creatures. Unfortunately this combination has resulted in the emerging sport of "wanging" or possum carcass tossing, a strange pastime that, unsurprisingly, has attracted much criticism in some quarters.

Certain areas of both North and South Islands can be described as 'un-crowded' encouraging some of the rural residents to move nearer to the few cities to talk to people rather than sheep or even possums.

SITTING COMFORTABLY

In early March we set off in search of people, possums and then, of course, some cricket. Our change of tour company was a good move. Already things were better than the previous year as Stuart and I managed to set off on the same plane. However my optimism faded when I took my seat. It seems I am destined to be cursed by HBS or "huge bloke always sits next to me" syndrome. Even paying the extra for business class was not enough to fully protect me against HBS. This chap's call for the extended seat belt was met with a sharp appraisal from the cabin steward who politely replied, "I think we may need two belts, sir".

I was interested to see that Singapore Airlines had re-modelled their business class seats in order to make more efficient use of cabin space. Selecting the flatbed option meant that the bottom of the bed cleverly disappeared into the seat in front. I played around with this for a while and then became rather curious to know how my huge neighbour would manage this feat. I could not see how he could possibly get all (or even part) of his substantial body into such a small space. Part of me was quite excited by the prospect of witnessing a passenger becoming jammed in the mechanism, but he must have shared my vision, as he stayed upright for the whole of the 12hr flight to Singapore. I did start to feel for the chap as his size was clearly a disadvantage on such a long flight.

MAKING THE MOST OF OUR STOPOVER

We had about 14 hours between flights in Singapore. Before we left home my friend Ian suggested that Stuart and I book into the Transit Hotel at Singapore airport. This turned out to be a valuable piece of advice and a great idea as a few hours rest was well worth the room rental. We also opted for the free two hour sight seeing trip around the city which was both interesting and a good use of our time. It included a short boat trip and a drive past the famous Raffles Hotel.

The short tour gave us a taste of the clinically clean city but not enough to fully appraise its attractions. As the time approached for the next leg of our journey we decided that the best way to keep ourselves awake would be to check into the free cinema, the only disadvantage being the darkness and boring, sleep-inducing films. They weren't even B movies, more like ZZZZZZZZZ movies.

FIRST CLASS SERVICE

After leaving the sleep inducing cinema we were eager to get on with the journey. My luck seemed to have improved as we boarded the plane for the Singapore to Auckland leg. Fears of further HBS were immediately assuaged by an unexpected upgrade to first class. It was nice to have even more space and attention although I declined the free pyjamas, particularly after seeing them modelled by another passenger. It was all very impressive but I couldn't really see the value of paying such a huge premium to be right up front.

CITY OF SAILS

At last, after what seemed to be many days in the air we arrived in Auckland and were met by our tour director, Martin.

Stuart and I were impressed from the outset. He soon had us settled into the comfortable Stamford Plaza Hotel and later organised for us to meet with a few of the other "single" chaps for beer and nosh. They were a friendly bunch and we all seemed to get on well. This early attempt to introduce us to each other was a very different experience from previous tours and led to some real bonding as the tour progressed.

NOT A VERY CROWDED HOUSE

Our first full day tour in Auckland was an interesting mixture of beach and bush. The breathtaking scenery included an elevated view right across Auckland from Mount Eden down to the black sandy beach. Even I couldn't resist a paddle in the Tasman Sea as the sun shone brightly. On our way back to the hotel we were shown where the New Zealand band Crowded House had their recording studio. Unfortunately no one was at home.

At night the whole group assembled in the hotel reception ready to be taken to the Auckland Yacht Club for our Welcome Cocktail Party. This was a good opportunity to meet the rest of our tour group as well as devour a few vol-au-vents and quaff the first of the many glasses of Sauvignon Blanc that would be enjoyed during the tour.

BACK OF BEYOND

Unfortunately we were not able to "take the weather" with us (apologies to Crowded House fans) as we travelled the next day by coach to Hamilton where we were greeted with heavy rain. However, when the rain subsided we did manage to watch the England team practise in the nets at the cricket ground. The highlight of the afternoon was watching reserve wicket keeper Phil (the "Colonel") Mustard being struck by a ball on the nose! It looked pretty nasty. We were later informed that he had recovered although he didn't play in any of the Tests.

In the build up to the cricket, the general air of excitement was being somewhat dampened by the rain. We hoped it would not persist as there seemed very little else to do in Hamilton. Some of the group had however noticed a particular building that we would pass on our way to the cricket ground every day. The frontage was emblazoned with "Girls! Girls! Girls!". Our tour guide reliably informed us that it was a brothel, which, somewhat surprisingly, are legal in New Zealand. Now better informed we of course just walked on by.

THE SUN COMES OUT TO PLAY AS THE CRICKET BEGINS

Hamilton has a population of about 160,000 but at the time of our visit only seemed to have two decent hotels. Ours, the Novotel, was fine except for the fact that we had to share it with both cricket teams. Our initial excitement at celeb spotting over breakfast coffee soon gave way to frustration. They descended en masse like a swarm of locusts ready to devour any food in sight leaving us more reserved Brits to make do with slim pickings. After two days of this, we made a pact to set our alarms early and get there before they came down to hoover up all before them. There was one exception, the English batsman Owais Shah, accompanied by his wife and young child, who behaved impeccably on a separate table.

Even in the dining area there were signs advising us what to do in the event of an earthquake. You would expect this in a country prone to shifting plates. However, I was not sure how helpful these instructions would be when we found ourselves perched high up in row T of a temporary stand at the somewhat quaint Hamilton cricket ground, Seddon Park.

OUR GROUP FORMS

A poor start inevitably led to us lying a distant second in the cricket but there was still much to enjoy and be distracted by during the days play. Virtually from day one of the tour Stuart and I settled into a group of like-minded chaps who were on their own. Some of the singletons had been paired up in rooms by the Cricket Tour Company to avoid paying the single supplement.

Richard, a retired chemist from Wilmslow was given the task of making sure the wine was measured out both accurately and equally. He was sharing a room with Ben, a lad in his 30s who, despite being considerably younger than the rest of us, mixed in well. Ben and his late father had planned to make this trip for several years, but Ben was forced to make the trip alone and was here remembering his father's love of the game. Apart from cricket Richard and Ben had a common love of Oysters. They were added to almost every evening meal. I tried them at one point but remained unconvinced that they were worthy of the "love".

Then there was "Ralph" (name changed to avoid offence and legal action). Ralph sat in the cricket stand directly in front of Stuart and I. He was obviously aware of the damage a day sat in the New Zealand sun could do. Not one to take risks, before play commenced on the first day of the Test match Ralph began to meticulously apply heavy duty, high factor protective cream to his arms and legs. He then moved to his face and as he lathered on the cream he began to take on a rather ghostly appearance.

He was very thorough but curiously, once his face was covered he stopped slathering and placed the remaining cream back in his bag. His bald pate remained completely unprotected in the fast approaching midday sun. Surely a hat must appear? It didn't. Stuart and I looked at each other; Richard and Ben exchanged knowing glances. No one said a word but we all watched as the colour of the exposed skin on his head gradually changed from white to pink to red until eventually an unmistakable purple hue was present.

Ralph remained engrossed in the play without reaction to his sunburnt pate, but we knew he must be suffering. The next day Ralph and hat appeared together and remained inseparable for the rest of the match.

THE LIGHT PROGRAMME

I have always enjoyed listening to the cricket commentary and found it compensated for my partial loss of vision. During the trip we were told that the radio commentary was on AM for the listeners across the whole of New Zealand. However, we also discovered that at Seddon Park we were able to pick it up on the much clearer FM signal. Much to our joy, the commentators did not seem to realise that when they went to adverts on AM people at the ground could still hear what they were saying on FM. This led to much amusement as they made reference to the direction of Harmison's "arse" followed by a discussion about his career being over. These regular lapses kept us entertained as England struggled on the field of play. I doubt the commentators shared our amusement when, rather late in the day they learnt of their errors.

Further fun was provided by the Barmy Army (BA) who came to life at about 4.00pm each day as their beer intake started to take effect. They had "composed" a new song for the Tour, which claimed that the New Zealand skipper, Vettori, was Harry Potter in disguise as, unusually for cricketers, he wore glasses. The BA's very own Jimmy Saville lookalike was chosen to conduct the singing, much to the disbelief of the locals.

IN THE SLOW LANE TO DEFEAT

New Zealand had started well posting 470 with Taylor reaching his first test century. England made heavy weather of their reply taking 173 overs to reach 348. We were glad of the radio distractions providing some excitement.

It looked like a draw until Sidebottom tore through the home side taking his match total to 10 wickets and leaving England 300 to win on the last day. But Mills took 4 early wickets and England collapsed to 110 all out with only Bell (54 not out) showing any resistance. Not good.

We soon got over the disappointment of the cricket. In fairness we were well beaten and our confidence was low as we prepared to move down to Wellington for the next match. We did think of having a whip round towards Harmison's return air ticket but decided he should stay and suffer with the rest of us.

HADLEE A HERO

As often happens on these trips we had a celebrity evening at the hotel. Famous New Zealand all rounder Sir Richard Hadlee was the guest speaker this time. A fantastic bowler and very useful batsman he was a joy to listen to as he recalled both his Test days and his success with Nottingham. He produced a signed bat to raffle, which I duly won. Not wanting to carry it half way across the world I gave it to one of our party, Jack Yardley from the Isle of Man, who was keen to use it raise money for a charity back on the island. I didn't know it at the time but he was raising money for a care home that my aunt Joyce, who lived on the island, would move to a couple of years later. A real win-win.

A ROYAL FLUSH

As a change from cricket our tour director Martin organised a quiz at the hotel (well you can't go clubbing every night), which our team won. Stuart's history knowledge was a big help, aided by a very knowledgeable young Ben. However it was a little embarrassing to find us only scoring three out of ten for the cricket round yet achieving a perfect ten in the Royal Family round!

RALPH'S ROUND

With the cricket in Hamilton over, we boarded our coach and drove to Tauranga on the coast, in the Bay of Plenty for a two night stay at the Sebel Trinity Wharf Hotel. On the first evening our small group met up for dinner. It now included Ralph, whose head had at last turned a healthier looking golden brown. We had been taking it in turn to choose the dinner wine each night and now it was Ralph's choice. He took full advantage of a shared bill by selecting the most expensive bottle on offer. Mind you, it was very nice.

A free day followed, and the boys decided to walk around the area in the pleasant sunshine. There wasn't a lot else to do so we declared the Bay of Plenty to be incorrectly named. At least our day of walking made up for five days of inactivity at the cricket.

VISITING A COUPLE OF OLD GEYSERS

The following day we were back on the coach on our way to Rotorua. We were left unmoved by our first stop, a demonstration of sheep shearing (well you shear one sheep.......). And of course you can't visit New Zealand without creeping up to view a caged Kiwi bird. Being nocturnal, they spend most of the daytime asleep. It was not surprising that we found it difficult to spot one in the enclosure when they are so small and immobile. Their most impressive claim to fame is that they lay the largest eggs of any bird in proportion to their size. We didn't see any of their eggs either.

There was a little more excitement at the Thermal Reserve, as you would expect with the sulphur smell hanging over the area. Nevertheless I remained fairly unimpressed by the geysers and mud pools partly due to seeing them many times on television, and partly because they are just not exciting!

This rather mediocre day was followed by "the Maori evening". It was marginally more entertaining if a little over staged (he says tongue in cheek, not out of mouth). It was more like a theme park attraction. There was singing and dancing, but I am not sure it did the Maoris much good to be shown in such a light.

BAR ROOM BANTER

Despite the enforced entertainment we had great fun whilst travelling. The group were good company and all enjoyed a regular supply of Sauvignon Blanc. Bar room discussions varied considerably in quality and depth: from trying to name the stars of 1960's Candid Camera; to the relative performance of hotel irons (I kid you not). It took a couple of hours for me to come up with Jonathan Routh of CC fame. I had nothing to add on the state of the irons other than to smooth things over when it got a bit heated.

The hotels on the tour were very good quality and well situated, but after staying in so many in such a short space of time we grumpy old men had perfected the art of boring people rigid on new topics such as the need to standardise the programming of hotel safes, and the drawback of ultra modern sinks. For those of you who have the stamina I will illuminate.

As far as sinks go, the variation of plugs led to the permanent disabling of at least one. In two hotels one flat metal plug popped up when pushed down, and popped down when pushed down again, and then pushed again to open. The other hotel had a plug that could only be released by spinning clockwise. Well being easily confused, at least one of us muddled the popping and spinning until inevitably the one to be spun was pushed, never to return!

Alternative sink discussions included questions as to why certain trendy sinks have no way of stopping the soap continually sliding back into the bowl. This flummoxed us so answers on a postcard would be gratefully received.

WELLINGTON TO BOOT

After one night in a log cabin at the Millennium Hotel in Rotorua, we boarded an early morning flight down to Wellington at the foot of the North Island for the second Test match. Here we stayed at the Holiday Inn located in the centre of the town. We wasted no time on arrival as we were immediately taken on a tour of the city followed by a guided tour of the Te Papa Museum. It was a well laid out modern building detailing the history of the Maori people and their Islands. There were lots of interactive exhibits, but I was glad there wasn't a test at the end as I would have failed due to the sheer volume of information.

NO SINKING AT THE BASIN

Sunshine greeted us at the Basin Reserve Cricket Ground. Unexpectedly, England were soon on top in the match and seemingly unhampered by the strong wind which blew around the ground. It's no wonder Wellington is called the "windy city". Despite the sunshine the cool wind drove almost everyone from the shady reserved seating to warm in the sun. This led to all the unreserved seating in the sun being occupied which in turn led to the gates being closed early leaving hundreds of reserved seats unoccupied in the main stand. A bizarre situation with many cricket lovers locked out of the ground unnecessarily.

VICTORY BECKONS

After three days of exhilarating cricket, New Zealand needed to score the highest number of runs on record in order to win a Test match. Given my previous inability to correctly forecast the outcome, I considered placing a bet on England losing but wisely thought better of it.

England's progress had been helped by England fan Billy the Bugler. He entertained the crowd with much needed additions to the Barmy Army repertoire, particularly the Harry Potter theme tune whenever Vettori came on to bowl. When England had a bit of a collapse he played "Memories" Billy was undoubtedly a hero.

We witnessed a great knock by Ambrose to complete his maiden Test century in only his second Test match. There was terrific swing bowling from Anderson in the first innings and Sidebottom in the second innings that led to England completing a convincing 126 run victory.

It was just as well that I had resisted the call of the betting shop, which was not surprising as this was not a pastime I pursued. One chap on our tour had followed the England cricket team to five different countries and this was the first time he had seen them win. At times our fielding was very frustrating with the number of chances missed it felt as though we had to get them out twice! Broad and Anderson had come in to replace the disappointing pair of Harmison and Hoggard. Broad looked like a developing talent, and Anderson's ability to swing the ball sealed his place in the team.

Away from the cricket, a highlight for me was meeting up with John and Aileen Stoker, good friends from back home. They were on holiday touring NZ but had found time to meet us at the cricket. It was great to see both them and England's victory.

POSSUM COUNT

The cricket was over but there was still so much to see and do before leaving this fabulous country. I had lost count of the number of coach trips at this point. Each coach driver we encountered liked to give us a run down on the locality, and the country as a whole. We had been told on every coach trip that there were at least 50 million possums in NZ (it's a fact, that's the thing). We came to the conclusion that this fact must be the answer to Question 1 of the coach drivers' driving test. Apparently, the possums had been originally imported from Australia for their fur. Some escaped and bred rapidly. This happened for two reasons: firstly there are no natural possum predators in New Zealand; and secondly back in Australia they ate eucalyptus leaves, which reduces their fertility. Not so in New Zealand as they continue to thrive.

LAST STRETCH

After Wellington our merry group disbanded as some of us had opted to fly down to the South Island to extend our trip rather than fly directly home. On our last night we assembled for a farewell meal at a restaurant we had coincidently visited a couple of days before - The White House, so called due to its painted exterior rather than the presence of an oval office. It was just as enjoyable as the first visit but with the atmosphere enhanced by the presence of the whole tour group. There were some great places to eat with very little increase in the cost as you move up in standard. The White House was amongst the most highly recommended, but hardly any more expensive than some of the more modest restaurants.

By now we had adopted 'Ralph' - of Hamilton burnt head fame - who fervently followed us everywhere particularly to bars and restaurants yet had managed to get away with only buying one round in sixteen days. We weren't sure if he was suffering from sunstroke, which had somehow affected his ability to speak up or find his wallet. By now we were amazed at the number of imaginative ways he could get out of a round and discovered his skill at avoiding paying was truly masterful. On our last day he joined us for the meal and spoke up…only to tell us what a great time he had enjoyed and how wonderful our company had been. He went home the next day although we fully expected to find him in the bar in Queenstown on the South Island.

REMARKABLE SOUTH ISLAND

Well in the interests of balance I have to report that 'Ralph' did buy the first round on the last night, but he also managed to vanish never to return at the end of the evening when it would have been his turn again.

I was forced at this point to apologise to several friends and family from back home who had been following my blogs as I sent out a blank text in the middle of the night and received several concerned messages by return. I had left my phone on at the cricket and must have sat on it a few times. A special big "sorry" was sent to Rick Firth (from Chapter 1) who was woken by at least three text alerts at 4am UK time

A BIT OF A FARCE

The larger group of thirty five had now split and after saying goodbye to our pals, Stuart and I became part of a smaller travelling band of fifteen. We were a little sad to see both Richard and Ben leave as they had proved to be a great double act, but the group soon took a new shape. Unbeknown to us at the time, it wouldn't be too long before we met up with Richard again on future tours.

In a group of thirty five it was inevitable that we would encounter some larger than life characters and we certainly did. Pay attention because this bit gets complicated. Harvey and Sally were travelling as a couple (i.e. staying in the same room). They used to be married, but were now divorced. Harvey had a partner in the UK. Sally was American and had no current partner. Harvey liked cricket; Sally is an American! Harvey wanted to come on the tour with his UK partner, but she didn't, so his former wife Sally was invited. Harvey's partner was apparently not too impressed with this arrangement and naturally checked on how things were progressed throughout the trip.

Still with it? Enter Graham, a divorced Pom, living in Melbourne near to his grown-up children. As soon as he discovered that Sally and Harvey were not a "proper couple" he invited unattached Sally to join him for dinner. "All perfectly above board" I hear you say, and it was, but of course it took the rest of the group a while to establish the facts. For several days tongues wagged, fingers pointed, people whispered and speculated with glee. Graham took it all in his stride enjoying his new found gigolo status, but it was all sorted in the end with no harm done and everyone happy.

The flight from Wellington to Queenstown went smoothly and our somewhat shrunken group booked into the Novotel Queenstown under our new guide, Sue, who had taken over the reins from Martin. We were right on the edge of Lake Wakatipu with the Remarkables mountain range as a back drop. Stuart and I took the Skyline Gondola cableway on the first evening and appreciated some fantastic views of the lake below, followed by a reasonable meal in the restaurant that reminded me of a motorway service station.

Queenstown is an amazing outdoor adventure centre which I thoroughly enjoyed, if enjoyed is the right word for being terrified on a jet boat Shotover, and a 4x4 trip to visit the Lord of the Rings sites. I am not sure which was more frightening.

The jet boat set off at high speed and was steered straight at the rocks only to be pulled away at the very last second. This happened time after time as we moved down the shallow river. The driver's ability was continually tested as were my nerves. Fortunately both passed the test.

I thought the drive to visit the film locations for the Lord of the Rings would be quite straightforward. It wasn't. The so-called highlight was the drive along a single track with a rock face on one side and a sheer drop of at least a hundred feet on the other. I was panic stricken as I don't do heights. The view across the landscape was, I am told, spectacular but I had my eyes closed for 99% of the time.

The track went on for a couple of miles and we were told that a mother has to bravely drive along it every day to take her young children to school. There were only a couple of passing points. I was relieved when we were back on normal roads. I couldn't identify any of the locations from the film, which meant it was a bit wasted on me.

For much needed respite from such 'exhilaration' we stopped to view the site of the completely mad (in my opinion) practice of bungee jumping. Why anyone would want to manacle their leg to a large piece of elastic and hurl themself into a canyon is beyond me.

That evening we boarded the 1912 vintage steamship TSS Earnslaw for a 40 minute cruise to Walter Peak Farm. A good meal was followed by a surprise as the room was cleared ready for our 'entertainment'. Could it be a band? A comedian? A juggler? No it was ..... you've guessed it.....more sheep shearing. You definitely *can* have too much of a good thing, so Stuart and I retreated to the gardens. By the time we got back on the boat the alcohol had taken effect and as a chap tinkled the ivories, we were all moved to sing an assortment of old songs increasingly loudly all the way back to the steamer's wharf.

SOUND AS A POUND

The next day we went to Milford Sound. The scenery at the fiord was spectacular but it took us over five hours to get there. Unbelievably it took our driver 2hours and 47 minutes to mention our friend the possum - a new record.

The Japanese were out in full force at Milford Sound. I had thought their economy was in a worse state than ours. Their happy smiling faces were everywhere. They love to snap away and it is almost impossible to take a clear picture of a view as they insist on taking group pictures in front of anything and everything.

The weather was unsettled but the boat remained stable in the protection of the fiord. I am sure the experience would have been even more enjoyable on a sunny day.

We had originally booked a flight back to avoid spending 10 hours of our day on a coach but the cloud was too low, so we endured another five hour journey back to Queenstown. Fortunately, there was no further mention of possums.

When we finally arrived back at our hotel I switched on the TV and caught CNN discussing the HBOS crisis. As my former employers they were now paying my pension. Even though it was Good Friday I hoped that my wife Sue was already outside our local branch of the Halifax forming an orderly line of savers. I also hoped Ian Stewart (a former colleague) would have a full explanation for me when I returned home. After all there were hopefully more cricket tours to fund!

CHRISTCHURCH AND HOME

The following day we were off to Christchurch. On our way we stopped off at Mount Cook to view the stunning scenery. The statue of Sir Edmund Hilary, the famous Everest mountaineer, outside the visitors centre has a wonderful backdrop provided by the Southern Alps.

Christchurch is the oldest city in New Zealand and the third largest with nearly 400,000 inhabitants. We had two relaxing days at the Crown Plaza Hotel with no formal itinerary. Stuart and I spent our time meandering around the town visiting the cathedral, botanical gardens and riding the renovated tramway. It is sad to think that our hotel in Christchurch was badly damaged, along with much of the city a couple of years later, by the 2010 Canterbury earthquake. Around half of the 185 people to lose their lives were in the TV tower, which caught fire.

I loved New Zealand's beautiful scenery, even if I was a little 'sceneried-out' by the end of our 24 day tour. The trip was enormous fun thanks to the great characters in our group. The Cricket Tour Company guides were exceptional, organising us, providing us with good hotels and an excellent itinerary. The cricket was mixed but always interesting.

CHAPTER 7 JAMAICA January 2009

Many people tried to put me off going to Jamaica, but the chance to avoid the worst of a British winter and watch cricket in a country that I had not previously visited was too much to pass up. Stuart, my usual cricket buddy, was not available for this trip but I planned to meet up with Richard who we had befriended on the New Zealand trip. Richard was travelling with his cricket pal John, so I knew it would be fun.

THE COUNTRY

Jamaica is almost 4,700 miles from home with a flying time of just over nine hours. The island is bigger than commonly thought being 146 miles long and varying between 22 and 51 miles wide. It is roughly half the size of Wales, and sufficiently large to warrant two airports.

One couple joining the tour decided to book their flights with Air Miles, independently of the travel company. Unfortunately they, like many, didn't realise that there are two airports: Kingston and Montego Bay. We were staying in Montego Bay and they flew into Kingston on the evening of our first day. It took them several hours to get to us, arriving in the middle of the night. They avoided the problem on the way back as we later moved to Kingston for the cricket.

There are some things you may not know about the island and its inhabitants. Jamaicans love their cell phones, recording a subscription rate of 107%, comfortably higher than the 98% subscription in the US.

It can snow in Jamaica. Hard to believe but the Blue Mountains at over 7,000 feet occasionally get a dusting, mainly of frost and sleet rather than the proper stuff.

Jamaicans are very religious with the majority being protestant Christians. They have the highest number of churches per capita in the world.

Jamaica doesn't just boast beautiful scenery, but having the third highest number of winners of the Miss World contest, behind Venezuela and the UK, it can also boast a pretty face or two.

OFF WE GO

As the flight from Gatwick was at 9.00am on Saturday morning I decided to take the sensible option and stay overnight at the Gatwick Hilton using my recently acquired "VIP" Hilton card, obtained by swapping some unwanted air miles. After checking in I made my way to the top floor and on exiting the lift noticed the sign for the executive lounge. I wandered around the corridors following my room number and the numerous reminders for the executive lounge. Having found and settled in to my room I looked around and saw the notice for, you've guessed it, the executive lounge and the enticement of free drinks and canopes, available to guests for the next hour.

I could not resist and wandered off to the lounge and proudly presented my room card, only to be told that I was not in an executive room and therefore not eligible to partake in the freebies. It looked pretty posh to me but then the standard of hotel rooms is rising. No problem, I produced my brand new Hilton VIP card. I was then told that the card did not allow entry BUT it could entitle me to an executive room that in turn would enable entry. At this point I ran out of enthusiasm and returned to my 'pretty posh' standard room and eventually resorted to room service.

FIVE MEETINGS WITH AN OLD BOSS

After a good night's sleep I was ready to fly to the sunny island. The flight over was good with the highlight being when things became a little heated down in steerage when after five hours of a nine hour flight it was announced that the booze had run dry. Things remained calm up top as the drinks continued to flow.

Immigration at Montego Bay airport has to be experienced to be believed. I was the first of our party to make it through to baggage reclaim in two hours fifteen minutes. The record for two of our group was just over three hours!

A small digression for Halifax/HBOS readers. On entering the immigration hall I found seemingly endless lines of frustrated tourists. I bumped into Mike and Louise Blackburn (Mike being the former CEO of the Halifax and my ultimate boss at the time). I actually bumped into them several times as the lines snaked back on themselves. I made the mistake of assuming that they were here for the cricket but Louise quickly put me right. I was advised that they were here to board a cruise. I hadn't seen either of them since Mike retired several years previously but typically he remembered me straight away and was on good form as usual. It was a happy distraction from the painful delay.

The scenes in the baggage hall were fractious. You would think that after such a delay all our bags would have been unloaded particularly as the screens were showing more recently landed flights. After being sent to the wrong carousel, I eventually found the correct one where the bags were still circulating, but it was now so overloaded with bags from subsequent flights that they were being flipped off the ends and forming huge piles. It was like those machines in the arcades that pile up the coins and then tip them over the edge.

There were plenty of staff there who seem transfixed by the sight and unable to move until a supervisor eventually managed to break the spell.

Our tour director, Clare, had introduced herself at Gatwick and soon had us on board our coach for the short ride to our hotel. My only association with the area was the 1970 one hit wonder "Montego Bay". Sung by Bobby Bloom and co written with Jeff Barry reaching number 3 in the UK charts. Sadly Bloom died at 28 when he shot himself cleaning his gun. Barry wrote scores of hits including Leader of the Pack, Da doo ron ron and Do wah diddy.

SETTLING IN

The first few days were spent at the all inclusive Riu Hotel in Montego Bay. The free drinks extended to bottles of spirits of well known brands in the bedrooms, which unfortunately lay untouched by yours truly. I don't do spirits as I prefer an occasional glass of cool lager any day. The food was good with a choice of restaurants to suit most tastes. The hotel was by no means full but what it lacked in atmosphere was made up for by the companionship of the group and the attention of the staff. We were well looked after.

I met up with Richard in the hotel bar and was introduced to his friend John (Peck). They had met on a Gullivers cricket tour to the West Indies and had remained friends. John was a retired headmaster and lived near Hull. The village in which he lived was very close to North Ferriby where we had lived when I was the manager of the Leeds Permanent in Hull from 1983 to 1985. Finding a common bond we all got on straight away and we still see each other at cricket matches from time to time.

Then after meeting John, the second new guy I met was Dave

who spookily lived in Solihull, about 400 yds from where my wife Sue and I were married. Dave was on his own and soon became an integral part of our gang along with Richard and John.

LIFE'S A BEACH

Drugs are a big problem in Jamaica and before travelling, I was warned that locals would easily spot tourists as potential buyers and I should particularly expect to be offered them on the beach. In the first few days both Richard and John spent quite a few hours on the hotel beach lapping up the sun. After a while I enquired as to whether they had been approached and offered any drugs. "Not once!" was the reply. I wasn't sure if they were relieved or disappointed to have been overlooked. As it turned out it was a private beach and therefore presumably off limits to dealers.

I am not really a beach lover but the sea did look tempting and Richard and John were clearly enjoying it. I decided to have a dip and carefully made my way across the beautiful sandy beach and stepped into the clear blue sea. I think it was my second step when I heard a deep voice behind me: "Respect man. Do want smokes, yeah man?". When I declined he smiled knowingly: "You had too many already? Yeah man." I just shook my head and hurried back to the apparent safety of dry land.

Those first few days on the island we enjoyed super weather and on the final day at Montego Bay I even risked a successful dip in the warm sea and equally warm pool. Most refreshing and thankfully there were no approaches from the "Yeah man" men.

The increasingly PC world we experience had not reached this corner of the Caribbean. There every sentence both starts and ends with "man" and the word "yeah" is added for dramatic effect e.g. "Yeah man, you having a great time, yeah man?" However, respect is also everywhere: "Yeah man I mean respect, yeah man".

NOT DUNN YET

After three relaxing days we moved across the island to Kingston stopping at Dunn's River Falls, a 900 ft waterfall which can be walked up as long as you don't mind holding hands with your neighbour so as not to fall over and get absolutely soaked. Great fun, especially when accompanied by the constant shouts of "Yeah man!" from the video man - DVD on sale for only $40 available immediately after your group returns to the locker rooms, including 15 minutes of Jamaican history and the exclusive backing music of the late but great Bob Marley. Our rep bought a DVD promising to send us all a copy. Still waiting!

FULL EMPLOYMENT

How many tour guides does it take to navigate you along the two roads from Montego Bay to Kingston? Answer: four. There was Gregory the driver (fair enough). Maxine the local tour guide who spoke three languages including English, Creole ("broken English) and Patois (even more broken English). She did, however, slow the coach down to point out the turning for the village, 'Sherwood Content' where Usain Bolt the sprinter was raised. There was Maxine's unnamed assistant whose total contribution was to take up a seat on the bus. Finally there was little Alfie who loaded the bags at Montego Bay and unloaded them in Kingston eight hours later. You can understand the job creation given that unemployment in Jamaica at the time was 33%. They all smiled and added to our enjoyment of the long ride.

Richard and I were a little concerned that our new friend David was going to be the new 'Ralph' (Chapter 6 New Zealand) as he left us at dinner before the bill appeared as he was tired. Retiring early meant he avoided paying for food and drink, which was one up on Ralph. Surely an error? Watch this space.

STEADY START TO CRICKET AND DAVE OFF THE HOOK

Along with various warnings about beach based drug dealers we were informed that ganja is illegal in Jamaica. We were therefore astonished to see and advert for an organised trip to visit a marijuana farm. During the visit you would be invited to sample the crop. This wasn't a trick organised by the local constabulary to boost their arrest count, it was all perfectly "legal" within the "farm". Needless to say we didn't go, but remained intrigued.

The cricket started and our rep, Clare, decided that in view of the traffic and it being the first day of play, we should leave the Kingston Courtleigh Hotel ninety minutes before the scheduled start. The journey took eight minutes! We were so early that the gates were still locked. Being British we duly agreed that it is better to be early than late!

 Sabina Park is a super ground having been redeveloped for the World Cup, it stands comparison with most Test grounds. The food kiosks looked neat and very well organized, until of course you arrived at the front of the queue and asked for a cheese sandwich. In response, the employee leisurely leant across the neatly arranged bottles and packets to cut a bread bun in half. He then took a huge slab of cheese and began to shave off great chunks. Taking his time, he finally shoved the cheese into the bread, smiling in triumph as if he had just cooked a Cordon Bleu meal. All this was achieved whilst balancing the bread on top of the bottles and trying to appease the ever-growing queue. The whole thing was then roughly bundled into a serviette and abandoned amongst the bottles. "Yeah man".

The first day's play results in honours about even with KP (Kevin Pietersen) the saviour yet again with 97. Freddie (Flintoff) dug in for a controlled innings of 43 and Prior looked solid. It was not clear at that point how good the pitch was. We would soon find out.

That evening after the play finished the gang went out for a Chinese meal. Surprisingly it was very expensive with wine starting at £30 a bottle for a Hardy's chardonnay, which is twice the price we were paying at our hotel. Red Stripe beer soon became very popular. Dave paid, cleared his debt and restored our confidence. Definitely no Ralph!

Boycott was staying at our hotel and was his usual grumpy self. He was a great cricketer and is a first class cricket commentator but I really wouldn't want to share a holiday with him.

Due partly to my imperfect sight I always enjoy listening to the local cricket commentary. The only problem in Jamaica was that the local station suffered technical problems and we had to watch for a day and a half with the commentary running about 20 seconds behind the actual play. This gap gradually slipped to about 50 seconds. This may not sound a lot but to start with we were one ball behind for a bowler with a long run up, and nearly two for a spin bowler. Although I found this strange at first, I got into a rhythm, even secretly clinging to the vain hope that whilst watching an English wicket fall the impossible could happen and the action will be replayed differently when the radio catches up. Things got out of hand when the delay increased to two or three balls. I turned to my friends sitting behind me to share my frustration only to be told that they had discovered a correctly synchronised station hours ago. Richard found it first but failed to pass on the good news.

The cricket had been slow but strangely absorbing. There were only 180 runs scored on the second day. The nearest score according to our tour sweepstake was 242 so it was declared a "roll over". Not sure how well this went down with Jon, the holder of the 242 "ticket". Those that saw Lara score his world record 400 in Antigua can say "they were there", well now we can say we were there when the usually prolific Chris Gayle scored one run in an hour.

SAME OLD GEOFFREY

At the end of the third day all three results were still possible. This was the question I put to Geoffrey Boycott in the lift the following morning. Mister Happy shrugged his shoulders and replied, "I don't know, I just turn up". Sir Geoffrey unfortunately living down to his reputation.

In total contrast Jonathan Agnew had spent two hours with our group the previous evening. He conducted a very relaxed and informative Q and A session. We then got a couple of mentions during the next day's broadcast, well done Aggers, "Yeah man, respect!"

IT'S HIM

The next morning the award for best senior moment went to John Peck, Richard's friend, (not to be confused with sweepstake Jon). Whilst in the lift I noticed a tall chap, referred to as 'Gibbs' by his colleague. I thought this might be the well known former Windies spin bowler Lance Gibbs. In reception I asked John if he thought that the chap who was now sitting in reception was indeed the great man. "Definitely" said John "you can tell by the eyes". I felt reassured that my spot was correct, and went off to boast about it to a couple of other members of our group. Less than five minutes later John came over and announced: "You see that chap sitting over there, it's Lance Gibbs". At first, I thought he was playing some sort of joke, but when I said "Yes I know. It was me who told you" the look of total embarrassment on his face made it clear that this was indeed the great senior moment of the tour. To his credit he did manage to laugh, and I promised not to tell anyone else, a promise I kept for about thirty seconds!

ALMOST ONE FOR THE RECORD BOOKS

Well, well, well. What can I say? When England found themselves twenty three for 6 wickets my handy little Playfair cricket annual was searched to find the record low Test scores. I know the likes of Stuart Hardy, my friend in Birmingham, would know without looking, but us mere mortals needed the help. The only mitigating factor given our position, I reasoned, would be to witness a new record low England score. This would enable us to claim an original "I was there" moment. It seemed remote that we would witness the all time record Test low of 26 (New Zealand) but we stood a real chance of seeing England's lowest score to date, 45 (v Australia), or their lowest v the Windies at 46. These new records looked even more possible when Broad became the seventh wicket to fall at twenty six. Bizarrely I then found myself actually wanting England wickets to fall. But it was not to be. A recovery of sorts to finish on fifty one all out left me without a record and a sad sense of sheer embarrassment, both for the performance of the team and my inability to remain a loyal supporter. Shame on us both.

At least one of my teams won that day as Aston Villa triumphed to win 2-0 at Blackburn. Dave is a Villa season ticket holder so we were in a very good mood listening to the world service early in the play before all the wickets started to fall. Our joy was short lived.

JAMMING

Away from the cricket tension on the island was rising. It was Bob Marley's birthday. Yes I know he died in 1981 but in Jamaica he is close to a god and his anniversary is duly celebrated. We went to a very nice restaurant called Red Bones that had a selection of local food plus live music. It normally offered Jazz or Blues but due to the special day we were entertained by a Bob Marley tribute band. The food was great and we had our first bottle of Sauvignon Blanc. It was not quite on form with the New Zealand wines, but a very acceptable Chilean. The music was great except for one thing: two hours of reggae but no Bob Marley songs. Well none that the four of us recognised.

The first singer had recently been awarded second place in Jamaican idol, the local equivalent of the X- Factor; the second singer knew someone who had been to watch the recording! No that's unfair, they were all pretty good and kept us entertained until the wee hours.

COFFEE TIME

On our last full day we took an organised trip to the Blue Mountains and a coffee farm (not the ganja farm). They are the tallest mountains in Jamaica with a high point of 2256 metres (7400 feet). The surrounding area is known for its high quality coffee– Jamaican Blue Mountain – which is grown on the slopes above 2000 feet and served (for a considerable cost) at Betty's of Harrogate. The quality product commands premium prices on the world markets. We sampled the product and declared it to taste, well, like coffee.

The Blue Mountains are also where Island Records was first set up by Chris Blackwell back in 1959, when he was just twenty two. The project was funded by his parents. The visitor centre displayed interesting memorabilia from the many famous Island Record artists such as Spencer Davis, Emerson Lake and Palmer, Free, Cat Stevens, U2 to name just a few.

Blackwell started off promoting local ska performers but had his big break with Millie Small's "My Boy Lollipop" which sold over six million copies worldwide.

The trip was made all the more enjoyable by the company of Clare and John Ward (another one) from Luton. As we drank our coffee and chatted we discovered they are Luton Town football fans, which I just had to admire. "Yeah man, respect"! They were great people who we would meet again during our trip to Sri Lanka in 2012. Jamaica has great weather, interesting sites and wonderful characters. It was an excellent trip. Who needs cricket!

CHAPTER 8 SOUTH AFRICA January 2010

As my cricket buddy Stuart had missed out on the fun of Jamaica we decided to watch the next Test series in South Africa. The main tour group set off before us to enjoy New Year in the sun, but we were still out there in time for the Tests in both Cape Town and Johannesburg. In between these two Tests we had opted to explore the famous Garden Route. Our friend John (Peck) who I had met on the Jamaica tour opted to join us on the same basis.

The cricket looked promising with England going one up in the three match series after winning in Durban. The weather also promised to be preferable to the   whiteout we were leaving behind in Yorkshire.

BODIES EVERYWHERE

Our plane was due to take off from Heathrow at 20.35 so we opted to travel down country by rail. Joining the Edinburgh train at York on New Year's Day was to say the least interesting. As we boarded, Stuart and I had to   clamber over bodies strewn across various parts of the carriage in order to reach our seats. Throughout our two hour journey we were interrupted by intermittent moans of "never again" from the girl opposite. She spent the whole time face down on the table in front of us. Her cries of anguish were accompanied by the somewhat disconcerting sound of heads colliding with tables as young men passed in and out of consciousness. The only time we heard from the on board conductor was when he announced that "all toilets in standard class are now out of service". A sense of satisfying smugness crept over us as we began to realise that we were probably the only passengers in our carriage without a hangover.

ROCKING AND ROLLING

Much to our relief, Stuart and I were actually booked on to the same plane. This not always being the case, we no longer took such 'details' for granted. We even managed to blag Stuart into the Virgin lounge for a very pleasant pre-flight meal, plus four (yes four!) Haagen Daz icecreams. Well they were free and strategically placed in half a dozen fridges around the lounge. The temptation proved irresistible. Having had our fill of freebies we met up with John. Since our return for Jamaica we had met up occasionally at Headingly, the home of Yorkshire cricket.

The flight was pleasantly uneventful for me but Stuart found himself sandwiched between a large gentleman and a very nervous woman struggling to contain her fear of flying. Her anxiety was made much worse by a sudden bout of turbulence. This triggered an hysterical response that attracted the attention of virtually the whole plane. The cabin crew tried their best to reassure her, and her husband tried to calm her down by suggesting that she drink a glass of water. This 'remedy' was greeted with bemusement by Stuart and total disdain from the woman herself. Peace was finally restored some thirty minutes later when the turbulence ceased. Thankfully the calm lasted the rest of the journey.

DEJA VU

We arrived at the Cullinan Hotel situated close to the busy V & A waterfront, which is where I had stayed on my previous tour in 2005. We discovered that the rest of our party who had arrived before New Year were out on a day trip to the Cape Peninsula where the Atlantic and Indian Oceans meet. We settled in and started to relax in the warm sunshine, a welcome contrast to the snow we had left behind. As we had missed the first few days of the official tour it was soon time to enjoy the cricket.

RETURN TO NEWLANDS

It was great to be reacquainted with our tour manager Sue who we had first met in New Zealand. Her colleague Martin, who had also proved to be first class on the New Zealand tour was due to join us later. Newlands is my favourite Test ground and it was great to be back again. With Table Mountain as a perfect backdrop, and the mixture of modern stands and grassy banks, it is the perfect setting for Test cricket. The first two days of cricket left the match finely balanced with a slight advantage to South Africa. Jacques Kallis hit a typically attractive century before being caught behind off Onions for 108. Anderson was the pick of England's bowlers taking 5 for 63. England fell just 18 runs short of South Africa's total of 291, with Prior top scoring with 76 and Cook contributing 65.

This all changed on day three. We were in a superb hospitality box with fantastic views, great food and plenty to drink. The British fans were out in force, with an estimated ten thousand in the ground out of a crowd of sixteen and a half thousand. We met up with Stuart Hardie from back home who was just two boxes away. He was there with friends on a self-organised trip.

We had been watching the severe weather back home and could not believe the amount of snow the country was experiencing. The weather in Cape Town was also extreme; from mist and rain on day one, to a sunny 36 degrees on day two. The local paper blamed El Nino (the band of warm ocean wáter that affects the climate every few years) and we thanked the same for bringing bad light on day one, although this enabled me to win £100 on the sweep for accurately forecasting the total runs scored.

Both teams were staying at our hotel and being amongst the players added to our enjoyment. They were all pretty friendly; Matt Prior looked a good ten years older than his age; and Pietersen (KP) proved to be larger than life in both character and stature. He was absolutely huge and very friendly to the fans, always saying hello when passing or in the lift. Some of the WAGs were there too but perhaps unlike their footballing counterparts had also brought toddlers and grandparents along. The young Yorkshire spinner Adil Rashid was part of the touring party but seemed to spend a lot of time on his own.

He was also not getting on the pitch other than to supply drinks. Stuart and I thought this was not good preparation for a young talented player.

SITTING PRETTY

When not at the cricket we spent much of the first few days on the hunt for Stuart's glasses, last seen on his head in the bar on day one. When they were first missed Stuart turned the bedroom upside down. He then went back to the bar where he felt sure he had left them. After finishing my unpacking I decided to join in the hunt. I emptied the safe and searched the wardrobe without success. I moved into the bathroom and was carefully examining the contents of Stuart's wash bag when I noticed from the corner of my relatively good eye that Stuart was not downstairs in the bar, but perched on the loo looking somewhat intrigued by my actions. In my defence, it was a very large en-suite, and being partially sighted didn't help. I made light of the situation and retreated leaving Stuart to finish his ablutions in peace. The glasses did eventually turn up under his bed much to our joint relief.

GREAT CRICKET

What a game. What a finish! I have often been challenged to explain to none cricket lovers how a draw after five days' play could possibly be interesting, let alone exciting. Well this one had it all. As Strictly Come Dancing judge Craig Revel Horwood would say "A..maz..ing"! In their second innings the home side put on 447 for 7 declared. There was some excellent batting from Amla who scored a rapid 95, but this was put in the shade by a magnificent 183 from the South African captain Graham Smith. This set England an impossible 466 to win. Survival for a draw was therefore the order of the day for the England's batsmen.

We started well enough with the openers putting on 100 for the first wicket. But wickets fell and a South African victory looked a certainty. However, Bell faced 213 balls before being caught, leaving Swann and Onions to survive to the close and earn an unlikely draw. We were on the edge of our seats as we counted down the overs to our eventual safety and much relief.

The only downside to an otherwise perfect day was the incredibly poor quality of the local radio cricket commentary. They got pretty much everything wrong - player's names (even from their own side), the score, fielding positions etc etc. But among the best gaffs when playing for a draw, with only 20 overs left and England still needing more than 200 to win, were: "Do you think Strauss is still thinking he can win?"; and with just 26 balls left and Bell on 78..."Bell has just checked the scoreboard so I think he thinks he still has a chance of reaching his 100". We don't know how lucky we are to have great commentators such as Jonathan Agnew and Nasser Hussain

ON A PLATTER

As you may be aware seafood is pretty good in most parts of South Africa and the Seafood Platters (SFP) are excellent but also not cheap. We struggled to find one offered below £40 whereas fillet steak cost around £10 in even decent restaurants. Our friend John Peck had been given a recommendation for a great seafood restaurant called Panama Jacks, so we decided to give it a try. It was hidden away in the docks area of Cape Town. We were out as a group of about a dozen led by Sue our tour manager for the Cape Town leg from the Cricket Tour Company.

The restaurant was packed and there were one or two celebrities present, including Ian Botham who was there with his family. We took our seats and decided at the outset that we would divide the bill equally at the end of the meal. The lady next to me, who I hadn't spoken to before, ordered the very expensive SFP and a rather pricey starter. She then went on to order a good quality Sauvignon Blanc on behalf of us all. The group exchanged a few concerned looks but remained silent, as we Brits often do. However, to Stuart, John and myself she instantly became a marked lady and was from then on known as 'SFP'.

I attempted to engage SFP in conversation during the meal asking her which optional trip she planned to take between the Tests. "Victoria Falls" she replied. " Where are you flying to?" I enquired. "Livingstone" was her retort. "You presume!" I countered. "No. No it's definitely Livingstone" she insisted. Somehow I managed to contain myself. When the bill came and was divided equally as agreed, SFP didn't bat an eyelid as we all duly paid up. We did not warm to her and unfortunately this was not the end of my encounters with SFP.

GARDEN ROUTE

Martin was to be our tour manager for the second leg so as we left Cape Town we said goodbye to Sue and set off for the Garden Route. We made a couple of unscheduled stops along the way. Only cricket followers would understand our interest in the diversion to be shown where the disgraced South African cricketer Hansie Cronje met his fate. He died in a plane crash on Cradock Peak in 2002 at the young age of 32. A talented all rounder and former SA captain, Cronje was banned for life following his involvement in match fixing. There was little to see other than an imposing mountain peak. Further along the road we were brought to a halt by a troop of baboons crossing the right in front of us. It was a strange sight on a main road, or any road for that matter.

Our next stop was a scheduled visit to the Cango Caves. I have never been comfortable in confined spaces, and caves are fairly low on my list of "things to do". However, these were not ordinary caves, they had spectacularly high ceilings and were not at all claustrophobic. The paintings in the limestone caves were evidence of human habitation going back to the stone age. In the large open areas, I breathed easily and declared the visit an hour well spent.

GIDDY UP

I can't say I was excited by the prospect of a visit to the Safari Ostrich Farm, but how wrong could I be! It was both interesting and enormous fun, at least for us, although not for the poor ostriches. I find it hard to believe that ostrich riding is allowed in this day and age, but in SA it clearly is. There was some protection for the poor flightless birds as only those below eleven stone were allowed to sit on them. This ruled out all the men and perhaps should have ruled out one or two of the brave ladies who perched precariously on their backs before moving slowly around the paddock. I kept expecting the RSPCA to appear and halt proceedings, but they didn't. I was torn between laughter and pity. I think I was right not to start a book on the outcome of the three "horse" race as I am sure there would have been a steward's enquiry.

After the watching the poor things suffer we went on to eat them! Not the ones we had just watched of course. Ostrich tastes a bit like beef, with the flavour removed. Ostrich meat is very expensive as it is costly to produce, but it is thought to be beneficial for those seeking a low cholesterol diet. The skin is used to make wallets and bags, but again items are very expensive due to only small amounts being recovered from birds that fail to survive encounters with their jockeys. The gift shop sold small wallets for about £80. We didn't buy anything and rapidly moved on to our next venue.

TRUNK CALL

We had a couple of nights in the very pleasant town of Knysna staying at the Knysna Quays Hotel. We spent the morning of the second day at the local elephant park. A fascinating place, the park has provided shelter and food for orphaned elephants since 1994. We were encouraged to get up close and personal but this is easier said than done in elephant encounters. There were no fences but plenty of feces.as each adult elephant produces over 100lbs of dung every day. We learnt that the dung can be a useful mosquito repellent when set fire to, but there were no takers when small shovels were produced. It was interesting to see how these rescued animals flourished in such a caring environment. Some stay permanently and others are moved to different secure facilities.

ON THE BOARDWALK

Leaving 'Nellie' and Co behind we packed our trunks and headed for lunch at the Tsitsikamma Mouth Trail. The scenery was interesting particularly from the boardwalk that runs along the ocean. Strolling in the sun and looking out across the sea as if we had recently conquered new lands was a very relaxing way to spend the afternoon.

In the evening we were treated to a trip on the ocean, taking the sundowner cruise from Knysna. This was a very pleasant way to end the day and complete our trip along the Garden Route. I don't know what I was expecting from this part of the tour but based on reports form friends and what I had read I had high expectations. I enjoyed it a lot, but if truth be told I was still left slightly underwhelmed, as were some of my fellow travellers.

IN AND AROUND JO'BURG

We boarded our coach and headed to Port Elizabeth for our flight to Jo'burg. We had a couple of days to explore before the cricket was due to begin at the Wanders Stadium. This gave us time to get a feel for Johannesburg turbulent past with organised visits to the Apartheid Museum and the Soweto Township.

The Sandton Sun Hotel is situated a few miles outside Jo'burg, in a modern, upmarket area. On our journey from the airport our coach driver took us on a ride through the centre of the city. Some of the sights included old colonial buildings that seemed to have been left to deteriorate somewhat. The central Post Office building had a familiar façade but was visibly crumbling due to neglect. Probably the most interesting aspect of the trip was that our driver did not stop once, even passing through traffic lights when they were on RED! I think it was a case of our safety coming first in an area where robberies were common when traffic halted.

The next morning was spent at the Apartheid Museum. It was well laid out, informative and certainly helped our understanding of the many injustices suffered by so many, for so long.

Our last trip before the cricket started was a full day's tour of the Soweto Township. We saw examples of the housing projects that were at the centre of Mandela's campaign to improve living standards, and stopped outside the home of Desmond Tutu, and 8115 Vilakazi Street where Nelson Mandela had lived before his imprisonment. We also visited the site of the 1976 uprising against the enforced teaching of school children in Afrikaans, rather than their native language. On the first day of the uprising there were 23 fatalities. The protests brought international media attention to the problems of oppression in Soweto and galvanized support from world leaders who reacted with increased sanctions against the South African government.

There was some excitement when we were told we would be eating lunch at the "best restaurant in Soweto". It probably was, relatively speaking. Staff with happy smiling faces met our needs in full. We all enjoyed the day but I found it difficult to form a view of how the transition from such a harsh past to a new a new way of life was faring.

CRICKET RETURNS

The tension was beginning to build on the eve of the fourth and final Test of the series with England one up. Captain Strauss, Vice captain Cook, and coach Andy Flower were deep in discussion at the bar of our hotel. This gave us confidence that the planning was on track. The weather forecast was not good, with a chance of thunderstorms each day, but we were assured that the forecasters always said that. Mind you we had experienced a belter of a storm just after we had arrived so maybe there was truth in it.

As we entered the ground two things struck us: the size of the ground and the number of supporters. Where was everybody? The Wanders Cricket Ground can hold up to 34000 spectators, which is definitely one of the world's largest grounds, if you exclude Melbourne in Australia. Its size made the small crowd on the opening day look particularly dismal.

The really good news was that our pleas to be found private box facilities behind the bowler's arm had been successful. Fortunately Martin had found out that the firm that was responsible for the boxes at Cape Town was able to provide identical facilities at the Wanders for the same price.

ANOTHER 'I WAS THERE' MOMENT

It is very unusual to see a wicket fall off the very first ball of a Test match. Strauss's dismissal was the first time this had happened to England for more than 70 years. This was not a good start, and unfortunately it got worse with England all out on the first day for a poor 180.

As South Africa went out to bat, their captain Smith was very lucky to play and miss about six times before play ended on the first day. He also survived a clear snick to wicket keeper Prior. England's old "friend" Daryl Harper, the third umpire, struck again by not turning up his stump microphone to hear a clear nick, unlike the radio and TV channels. Add to this a dodgy "no ball" and you had one very unpopular umpire. Smith went on to make 105 out of a total of 423.

Just as things were looking really bad, the fateful thunderstorm struck. Starting immediately after lunch, incredibly it turned the ground into a lake in minutes, delaying play for over three hours. Even so I feared that extreme weather was not sufficient to save the boys.

SFP RESURFACES

Off the field, our old friend SFP was at it again making herself increasingly unpopular as she led a small but vocal protest at the standard of catering in our hospitality box. Her main complaint centred on the "poor food" on offer. She particularly objected to the cold lamb chops. I joined the discussion to try to assist our beleaguered tour manager, Martin. I insisted that there was nothing wrong with my chops, John's or Stuart's and really we should be grateful for such great hospitality. This didn't really help. "Were yours boiling hot then?" blasted SFP. I was tempted to say that an all inclusive box (all drinks and two meals, plus snacks) behind the bowler's arm for a cost of £50 a day, was exceptional value, but it was clear that the lady was not for turning other than towards another glass of G&T.

On the evening of the second day we were treated to an audience with Sky cricket pundit "Bumble" aka David Lloyd ex England player, manager and now Sky commentator. Known for his excitable style and catch phrases such as "start the engine" when a result seems close, Bumble was great fun. He kept us well entertained recalling his wide experience in and out of the game, and as a Sky presenter.

WALLOPED

Sadly our experience was all too quickly over at the Wanders Cricket Ground. In summary we were well beaten by the better side. Only Collingwood (47 and 71) and Swann (27 and 20 plus 2 for 93) came out of the match with any real credit. Failing to get passed 200 in both innings led to a crushing innings defeat.

The four match series ended all square but South Africa were by far the better side in both of the matches we witnessed. Like Newlands, the Wanders is a super ground that was sold

111

out on Saturday but virtually empty on the first two days. Being in excellent hospitality boxes for both Tests was a real treat. Well done Cricket Tours!

PILLOW FIGHT BREAKS OUT

Back at the hotel a pillow fight took place. I normally sleep very well but the first couple of nights I was restless and seemed to have developed a bit of a wheeze. At first I put this down to the high altitude (6000ft), but then my brain started to work and I realised it was the feathers in both the pillows and duvet to which I am allergic. I rang housekeeping expecting immediate assistance but it was then that the fight started.

Ding Ding, Round 1

"Hi, sorry to trouble you but I am allergic to the feathers in the pillows and the duvet. Can I please have foam replacements?"
"You want feather pillows?"
"No, I need to change the feather pillows I have for foam, or something other than feathers."
"I will send you some feather pillows."
"I am sorry, I am not making myself clear. I already have feather ones. I do not want feather ones, I need no feathers."
"No feather?"
"Correct, no feather."

You can tell that my polite language was beginning to break down into a more basic version of the mother tongue.

Seconds out, Round 2

We returned from the cricket to find new sheets on the beds, but, yes you've guessed, I still had feather pillows and duvet. I picked up the phone.

"I rang you yesterday asking for replacements for the feather pillows and duvet but you have sent me feather pillows again. I need foam."

"You want feather?"
"No. Me want NO feathers! Me want foam!"
"Ok we will bring them to your room, sir"
"Thank you"

Round 3

Hooray, foam appeared. A good night's sleep is enjoyed.

Round 4

The next evening at bedtime, expecting all was now well in the duvet department I drew back the cover, slipped into bed and to my dismay discovered that the feathers were back. I picked up the phone....down in housekeeping only the night staff were on duty.
"I have feather pillows again, I do not want feathers, I want foam."
"You want feathers?"
"NO! NO FEATHERS! Please bring me foam! Please bring me foam NOW!"

Some fifteen minutes later one foam pillow and one *double* foam duvet appeared for my (single) bed. I readily accepted them and slept well once my blood pressure had returned to normal.

Round 5

After another good night's sleep, I was more confident that the situation had been resolved. Our maid appeared at 8.30am to clean the room. She looked puzzled by the pile of pillows and sheets in the middle of the room and the double duvet piled up on my single bed. I believed that given the practice I had had, I could adequately explain the situation. I pointed at the rejected feather pile:
"These feathers. Feathers bad," (pull face and point thumbs down.
I turned to the foam pile on my bed:

"These foam, foam good." (smiley face and big thumbs up). The maid smiled. Not surprisingly Stuart looked embarrassed by my broken English. I indicated that the feather pile needed to go out of the door. The maid caught on and removed the offending bed linen. Cracked it. I retreated to the bathroom as the maid left saying she would be back later.

After my shower I returned to the room to see that she had left the feather pillows with covers removed. I took no chances and rushed to the door and threw the offending items as far as I could down the corridor. I won, on points, but there were still two nights left.

Thankfully all was well on the bedding front for the remainder of our stay. On reflection I feel more than a little uncomfortable at how I communicated to those poor housekeeping staff but really feathers can make it a struggle for me to breathe at times.

KEEP ON TREKKING

With the match finishing earlier than anticipated we had Monday and Tuesday to fill before flying home. Anyone who has been to Jo'burg will know that there is very little to see and do here once you have done the Soweto Tour and the Apartheid Museum. Only the gold mine and the brewery tour were left, both of which were closed on a Monday. We asked one local what there is to do in Jo'burg and he quickly replied, "Go to Pretoria". So we opted for a group trip as we still had the tour bus, which would have taken us to the cricket had we not been thrashed. I wasn't sure I would be able to sleep with anticipation, but at least I now had foam to sleep with.

To the south of Pretoria is the Voortrekker Monument, built to commemorate the Great Trek undertaken by the Dutch Afrikaans in 1837/8 to escape the rule of the British on the Cape and find a better life. It was a long and hard trek with many battles, the most notable being the Battle of Blood River in 1838. Outnumbered by the Zulus, the Voortrekkers won a huge victory that was a turning point in their struggle. Andries Pretorius, after whom the city was eventually named, led the victors. I was so taken with the account that I bought a set of commemorative stamps back in Sandton. At the equivalent coat of 50p it was a bargain.

Pretoria was quite interesting with many striking buildings due to its role as the executive part of the government and being the home of three universities. The foreign embassies located in the city ranged in their prominence, with the US building dwarfing all others.

With one day left at Sandton we checked the local cinema to see "What's on" and discovered it was showing the new Sherlock film starring Robert Downey jr as Holmes and Jude law as Doctor Watson. As we sat waiting for the main attraction to begin we noticed that the England strike bowlers Anderson and Broad had also come to see "What's on". We enjoyed the film and returned to our hotel to pack our bags full of nostalgia for London, England and home.

This tour was first class, even though it turned out we were second best in the cricket. South Africa is a fantastic country providing great things to see and do at affordable prices. What an achievement in spite of the continuing political problems.

CHAPTER 9 SRI LANKA March 2012

Things were a little different on this trip. Stuart, my regular cricket buddy, decided to join the tour for the two Tests in Galle and Colombo, but miss the first week's sightseeing. Our friends, John and Richard, who we had met on previous tours, and who usually shared accommodation, had similar ideas. The outcome was that Richard and I went out for the whole three weeks and shared a room for the first week. When John and Stuart arrived at the beginning of week two, we swapped roommates. I was happy with the arrangements, as I will share with anyone, my only concern was whether my snoring would bother Richard. Thankfully his ear plugs worked.

THE COUNTRY

Sri Lanka lies 900 miles south of India, over 5500 miles from home and over 12 hours flying time. There are many things you may not know about Sri Lanka. Known as Ceylon until 1972 it is the world's second largest exporter of tea behind Kenya. Back in the mid-1800s the country's main export was coffee rather than tea, until an outbreak of a fungus known as coffee rust forced the country to switch to tea. This in turn led to Britain moving to tea as the hot dink of choice.

It is a country of contradictions. Often found confusing is the local practice of shaking the head to mean yes. Equally confusing is the custom of calling restaurants 'hotels' when clearly there are no beds on offer. One might assume that the national sport is cricket, when it is in fact volleyball.

TOO MUCH MONKEY BUSINESS

Sunny Sri Lanka is spectacularly beautiful! The relaxing week leading up to the first Test was an enjoyable start to the trip as we became acquainted with the thirty or so like minded cricket lovers in our group. It included a number of people we had met on previous ventures, but thankfully no SFP (South Africa 2010) or "it must be my round" Ralph (New Zealand 2006).

The first week of sightseeing and sharing with Richard went well. No falling out, and no snoring problems. Our first hotel, the Jetwing Blue Resort, was not far from Colombo in a superb setting by the sea. We stayed there for two nights, really just to recuperate from the flight and acclimatise to the tropical weather. It was a great introduction to the country.

ENTERING THE TRIANGLE

On day three we set off on a sightseeing tour using the Cinnamon Lodge Hotel at Habarana in the heart of the Cultural Triangle as our first stop. This eco-style hotel was set in a woodland area close to a beautiful lake. The only real drawback was that we were sharing with a large troop of monkeys who were adept at stealing biscuits, often from right in front of you. They swung acrobatically above us as we dined in the garden restaurant. This was initially amusing but became a little disconcerting when a whole troop began closing in as we sauntered around the edge of the lake. We were advised to report any inflicted bites or scratches so that we could be rushed to the local hospital for rabies jabs. I am pleased to report that on this occasion none were required.

Our accommodation was spread around the property in spacious, air-conditioned chalets, each with individual terraces surrounded by trees and other vegetation. Our room was on the outer reaches of the hotel. Its somewhat hidden location made it a real challenge to find in the daytime, let alone in the dark. The outside lighting was pretty poor and coming back after dinner was difficult for those with 20:20 vision, so near impossible for me. Fortunately, Richard has perfect sight and a good internal compass, but we still got lost on more than one occasion.

Sri Lanka's 'Cultural Triangle' is outlined by three major Sinhalese cities: Anuradhapura in the north; Polonnaruwa in the east; and Kandy in the south. Threaded between these cites are World Heritage Sites displaying fascinating collections of Buddhist art and architecture, two of which we visited.

The first was the Golden Cave Temple of Dambulla. It is actually five caves that feature wall paintings by Buddhist monks. It is quite a walk up to the top, but well worth it with over 150 statues and many paintings. The second was Sigiriya a 5th century rocky fortress. We were advised to bring water and wear sensible shoes. An oxygen supply would have been even more useful for that climb! We followed this with a visit to the ancient ruins of the former capital at Polonnaruwa where many 11th and 12th century statues of Buddha remain. Well that was my cultural void filled for a while!

As in many other counties in this part of the world the local approach to driving is, shall we say, haphazard. It becomes even more 'interesting' when you are the last to board the coach to find only the front seat left vacant. A deliberate tactic by those in the know. Even our tour guide abandoned the microphone position in favour of the safer option of shouting from row 15!

For a short period, my lack of full vision was an advantage although not a sufficient one to overcome the lack of a seat belt. The good news was that I eventually discovered one end of a belt, which encouraged me to dig deeper and extricate the business end. Belted up, I began to relax a little and enjoy the scenery, which could be described as 'lush', but not in a Gavin and Stacey way.

LIKE TAKING KANDY

The next morning our group travelled south from Harbarana to Kandy. Being a little wiser Richard and I were first on the coach and able to bagsie the back seat. Our Kandy hotel, the Earl Regency, was perched on a hillside offering excellent views of the green landscape. As a creature of habit, on entering the room I immediately checked out the TV. Not so my travelling companion Richard. Within seconds he was stripped down to his Y fronts and purposefully heading for the small, but perfectly formed balcony to enjoy the view! He was immediately captivated as he stood looking straight ahead over the verdant landscape. However, his joy was rapidly replaced by shock as he became aware of a cacophony of titters and gasps from fellow guests on the unshielded balconies on either side who were no longer enjoying the countryside, but carefully checking out his credentials!

One of Kandy's highlights is the Temple of the Tooth Relic, an impressive and popular Buddhist temple that is best viewed at night. Our local tour guide, Akhtar, had an impressive knowledge of the area, which he eagerly shared with the group, only occasionally pausing long enough to take a breath. Inside the temple he carefully gathered us around him in the inner sanctum and began a fifteen minute explanation of its history. The only problem was that his latest lecture coincided exactly with the beginning of an offering by the monks. Their procession was accompanied by extremely loud drumming. So loud, that even those stood next to Akhtar could hardly hear a word. The drumming continued, as did Akhtar, and they seemed to be level pegging but then the Buddhists got the upper hand as the local equivalent of bagpipes, burst into life. Now no one could hear our man. Did he stop? Of course not. Somewhat unkindly sniggering broke out, but Akhtar was clearly a pro and carried on regardless.

Talking of musical instruments, there was an interesting discussion at the breakfast table one morning when we noticed a peculiar pan pipe type of whistle accompanying our meal. It was surprisingly tuneful and strangely did not seem out of place. Coincidentally that morning's conversation turned somewhat seriously to an incident at a hospital in Bristol where a surgeon had unfortunately developed a reputation for very poor results. It became quite an intense discussion about the role of whistle blowers! I suggested, as is my wont, that they (the whistle blowers) were becoming extremely common as there was even one here! Thank goodness our Cricket

Tour manager, Martin, was in tune with my sense of humour and immediately broke into a stifled snigger. Regrettably, the story teller, a rather intense bloke who shall remain nameless took a good deal longer to find the right note.

GALLE CALLS

On our way down to Galle in readiness for the first of the two Tests, we stopped off at the Pinnawala elephant orphanage. This popular attraction is run by the Wildlife Authority and was home to about sixty elephants. We arrived just in time to see the first of a twice daily routine of the herd bathing in the river. It is quite an event. The elephants parade down the road before they immerse themselves and appear to have great fun slashing and squirting water across the wide river. We were very fortunate to be ushered into an elevated riverside viewing area and offered drinks while we watched the lovely spectacle of young and old gently bathing and spraying each other.

We drove on to Galle for the start of the cricket on the Monday -whatever happened to Tests starting on a Thursday? Stuart and John joined us and usual room sharing was established.

Galle had been devastated by the Boxing Day tsunami in 2004 with many losing their lives. Amazingly our hotel survived, due partly to its open design that allowed the sea water to pass right through. Other areas of the town were not so fortunate. The cricket ground was severely damaged but was rebuilt and reopened in 2007.

THE CRICKET BEGINS…. AND ENDS

I won't spend long on the cricket, as England didn't spend much time on it either. Suffice to say, we lost. The difference was 75 runs in a relatively low scoring match. I can offer a few (lame) excuses.

Excuse number one:

It was hot (in fact very hot and humid) although it was the same for players on both sides.

Excuse number two:

The wicket was a bit dodgy. This is true, but again both teams had to contend with the problem.
Excuse number three:

The team had flown a long way and only played a couple of warm up games. Sri Lanka only flew in from Australia and India a couple of days before the test started and had only played a couple of one day games.

Excuse number four:

The team hotel was 1.5 hours' drive from the ground. This was the same for both sides due to a major error by the SL authorities making a very late booking. Our travel company (Cricket Tours) booked the hotel they usually use which is less than ten minutes from the ground and set in a beautiful position overlooking the Indian Ocean.

Excuse number five:

We lost the toss. OK I'll give them that one. Winning the toss is nearly always a significant advantage when playing in Asia.

Excuses aside it was a disappointing performance with only Trott scoring any runs in the match (112 in the second innings). This was Trott's seventh century but the first one to come in a defeat. Of the bowlers, the reliable Anderson took 5 for 72 in the first innings, and Swann 6 for 82 in the second innings. Sri Lanka's run machine Jayawardene tore the England attack apart with 180, which turned out to be 56% of the first innings' score. Poor English fielding led to him being dropped four times, twice by poor old Monty Panesar. But the

Sri Lankan batsman's 30th Test century was probably the difference between the two sides.

ON THE PLUS SIDE

The cricket ground at Galle is unique as it is guarded by the fort at one end and fringed by the Indian Ocean at the other. The Portuguese originally fortified Galle but the Dutch were responsible for the fort that stands today and is now a World Heritage site. Not surprisingly it is regarded as one of the most picturesque Test grounds in the world. It is also known to be one of the hottest.

I knew it would be hot but I have never been so grateful for sitting in an air-conditioned hospitality box. We were situated between the press and the TV boxes, we were so close we could almost see the join in Michael Vaughan's hair weave, and I am sure I heard Geoffrey Boycott's moan. I was fortunate to be situated near the only television set in the box. It was precariously balanced on an up-turned dustbin. We lost the signal several times as there was no plug on the power cable, just bare wires pushed into the socket. Sporadically they fell out and one of the three young "box boys" would risk a severe shock by using a ballpoint pen to force the wires back into the wall. I could hardly bear to watch. Health and Safety was yet to reach Galle.

Elsewhere in the box the beer was cool, and the wine was interesting. When did you last see a carafe of Paul Masson? I stuck to a moderate intake of beer, and plenty of water.

Security at the ground could best be described as disorganised, however, the presence of machine guns certainly kept us alert. A jeep containing a neat stack of unguarded rifles evidenced the local extreme yet inconsistent approach to security. In addition to our match tickets, we were issued with security passes each day but were never asked to produce them. Some days the guys on the door inspected our match ticket on entry, but on other days we were simply waved through.

After the match finished on Day 1 we returned to our hotel feeling more than a little downcast, but our spirits were soon lifted by the thought of taking part in Martin's special quiz night. John, Stuart, Richard and I combined our considerable brain power and despite being at least three points behind every team after the first round we pulled through to win by one point. To give you an idea of how bad we were, in round one Richard, who had lived in Melbourne for twelve years, confidently declared that Sydney was the original capital of Australia. Much to our amusement the answer was of course Richard's home town of Melbourne.

Never mind, we pulled through and the team proudly received top prize. Discussions quickly turned to what we 4 non-smokers could possibly do with six ashtrays bearing the hotel's logo. Plant pot drip tray was the winning suggestion, although there was some concern regarding the appropriateness of the rather porous material.

BACK TO NATURE

With the cricket finishing a day early, our group ventured off on a rapidly organised boat trip into the mangrove swamp. Following instructions, insect repellent was generously applied to all exposed areas. Whilst enjoying our boat ride we pondered whether poor old Monty (Panasar) would be kept behind in the England cricket camp for extra catching practice. He certainly needed it.

We saw lots of wildlife both on and off the water including kingfishers and kites. Chopping coconuts was a new experience, as was discovering the secret of growing cinnamon, which we were all told repeatedly must continue to be kept secret. This was mostly communicated through sign language, and thereby guaranteeing continued secrecy. As we passed a riverside temple I thought I spotted a stork, but quickly realised it was actually a statue. I never could tell Stork from Buddha! (apologies to younger readers and those intolerant of a poor pun).

Back on dry land we boarded our coach and headed off to Colombo for the second Test. Could the boys convince us, as well as themselves, that they deserved to hold the ranking of number one Test team in the world?

"ONE MORE THING": COLOMBO

Colombo is a busy city, and how our coach managed to avoid swallowing a tuk-tuk (known in Sri Lanka as a trishaw) is a mystery. Colombo is the Sri Lankan capital and home to over a million people.

Our hotels up to this point had been truly wonderful. They had beautiful settings, spacious rooms and fantastic staff. The overriding commonality was a sense of peace and tranquility. Then, Bang! We arrived in Colombo. The Cinnamon Hotel was huge with hundreds of rooms, plus many restaurants and bars. Boy oh boy it was busy. There were queues for everything. On arrival we wandered around trying to get our bearings and trying to book a restaurant for dinner. Everywhere seemed full, not helped by the closure (for refurbishment) of the largest restaurant on site. Great timing!

We broke from our quest at the coffee shop situated in the huge lobby area. Dozens of people swarmed around us. A piano on our left knocked out "I'm getting married in the morning". This was made even stranger when we realised that the pianist had more than a passing resemblance to the late Indian Prime Minister, Mrs Gandhi. Stuart summed up the situation, "It's just like sitting on Waterloo station". He was dead right, all it needed was a WH Smith's.

As a group of cricket buddies on tour we began to realise that we weren't getting any younger and the ravages of time were starting to take their toll on some members of the gang. John had become a little hard of hearing, I too, particularly in my left ear, and Stuart is so softly spoken that he could almost take up snooker commentary. This combination of auditory ineptitude has led to many amusing moments for example when I asked John if he had ever been to Betty's (the tea rooms in Yorkshire). He replied, "only on Grand National day". The thought of a betting counter in the genteel tearooms left us helpless.

A VIEW FROM THE BOUNDARY, ALMOST

On our way to the first day of the Test match we stopped to admire the R. Premadasa Stadium. It is huge, able to hold a capacity crowd of 35,000. This was the usual venue for Test matches but this year it had been decided that play would commence at the cosier P. Sara Oval to commemorate 30 years since the first Test between the two sides had been played at the smaller ground.

We arrived at the ground to find that the air con in our box had broken. Our super-efficient tour manager Martin immediately called for a technician. While we eagerly awaited his arrival, Martin invited people to enter, using a jocular style to lighten the mood and lessen our disappointment. Unfortunately, he said to one of the larger ladies in our group, "it's like a sauna in here, come on in and lose a few pounds". No offence meant, and fortunately none was taken and we all had a laugh.

Sri Lanka is a country, which presents the visitor with many surprises, but entering our box at the tiny Colombo cricket ground (capacity 4500) was slightly unnerving. Our guide, Martin, had warned us that things might not be quite the standard we were used to. Our concern was heightened when we discovered that the floor to ceiling glass frontage of our box was almost completely obscured by the side screen. Uproar ensued but fortunately calm was restored when the screen was moved to its correct position moments later. It is fair to say that we did experience a bit of a "wobble".

There were a number of soldiers patrolling the ground but security was, to say the least, lax. As I ventured from the safety of our box to stroll around the ground I noticed an army vehicle clearly marked "bomb disposal" parked next to a beer station. I wasn't sure if I was more anxious about a potential threat of a bomb, or the potential for the bomb disposal experts to be full of beer. With many England fans in close proximity holding their beer glasses I half expected to see a sign reading BEER DISPOSAL. I hurried back to the relative safety of the hospitality box.

That afternoon I was delighted to bump into John Clegg, an old school friend and former work colleague who was in the hospitality box next to ours. Now a retired district judge, John and his wife Chrissy were also on tour with a group of cricket fans including the actor Kevin Whately (aka TV detective Lewis) who was travelling with his son. I didn't get introduced but John and I chatted about old times and agreed to meet up when back home, which we have done at both Edgbaston and Headingly cricket grounds.

TWO MILLION NOT OUT

This match was very different from the one we had watched in Galle. Sri Lanka batted first after winning the toss and achieved a modest 275. Jayawardene scored yet another century that included the two millionth run in Test cricket. England replied with 460, which included a superb 151 from Pietersen with 6 sixes. Swann took 6 wickets as Sri Lanka set England a modest 94 to win on the last day. Fittingly, Pietersen finished the match off with yet another six. Our box was jubilant with hugs all round. This meant that England squared the series and hung on to their number one ranking in Test cricket.

MY HERO

Back at our hotel we decided to celebrate our victory and push the boat out by eating in the hotel's very impressive curry restaurant. It featured numerous interesting dishes from around the sub-continent. Sat alone on the table next to us was the former England cricket captain Tony Grieg. He was a bit of a boyhood hero of mine. As a young boy, my favourite cricketer was Ted Dexter. He was England's captain and played county cricket for Sussex. I therefore followed the fortunes of his county as well as my home county, Warwickshire. Although born in South Africa, Tony Grieg came over to England and joined Sussex in 1966 at the age of 19, scoring 156 on his debut. He was a tall, (6ft 6in) talented all-rounder. He went on to captain England and continue to play county cricket for Sussex. He naturally replaced Dexter as my cricket hero. He now worked regularly as a cricket commentator covering matches around the world. I toyed with the idea of inviting him to join us but he didn't seem to mind eating alone. A number of people interrupted his meal to ask for autographs. He was remarkably patient and obliging. We were impressed and left him in peace. Sadly, he passed away just 9 months later at the age of 66.

KNIGHT CAP

As usual there was a night at the hotel where a cricket celebrity was drafted in to entertain our group. This time it was the former England and Warwickshire opening batsman Nick Knight. His England career was most successful in the one day format where he averaged over 40 in 100 matches.

After the question and answer session had finished we moved outside for drinks and canopes. Nick Knight moved smoothly from group to group where he comfortably joined in conversations. When he came to chat with us conversation turned to his unusual middle name, Verity. He explained that he was named after a distant relative, Hedley Verity, who was a highly effective slow left arm bowler who played for

Yorkshire and England. He was highly rated and at Test level he took 144 wickets at an average of 24 runs per wicket. He was killed in action in Italy in 1943 at the age of 38.

After retiring from the game Nick Knight became a fine cricket presenter and was a thoroughly nice chap who went down well with our group.

A FEW LAST THOUGHTS ON SRI LANKA

In 2010 Sri Lanka had not yet introduced a legal minimum wage and consequently pay was generally very low and gaining worthwhile employment for many was a challenge. Not surprisingly, there was a very generous supply of labour within the tourist industry. Our trip benefitted from two tour guides, Martin and a series of local guides. We also had a driver and a bag boy who were with us for the whole of the three weeks. The bag boy must have had an interesting job description particularly, as we all took responsibility for our own luggage and not one bag was lost.

His other main role was to count the number of people on the coach, thereby making sure no one was left behind after a stop. This sounds sensible enough except he always started his head count after the main tour guide had checked us all off, and often after the coach had set off and was travelling in top gear. Funnily enough, he always managed to confirm a full bus.

The hotels also had plenty of staff; every lift area had a "greeter" whose only real challenge seemed to be keeping a sharp eye on the clock to know when to change his greeting from "good morning" to "good afternoon". They dressed smartly and were always polite and it was rather nice to be smiled at regularly.

We speculated that if a young Lift Area Greeter (LAG) did a good job over time they might eventually be promoted to the heady position of Front Area Greeter (FAG). If not they were destined to become an old LAG. The role of a FAG would perhaps be expanded to incorporate opening of the main door at the same time as offering an appropriate greeting, but as I discovered they also had other more discreet duties. As I was ushered through the front door one morning, the smartly dressed greeter (in full morning suit, including white gloves) muttered something to me that I didn't quite catch. As I paused to wait for the others, the diligent greeter left his post at the door, sidled up to me and discreetly pointed with his immaculately gloved hand to my fly area. Yes, I was at half-mast (actually, no mast at all). Job well done!

Despite the luxurious image presented to tourists, elements of poverty were still obvious. It would be hard not to notice the number of stray cats roaming the streets. Not being much of an animal lover Stuart considered the obvious solution would be for the local equivalent of the RSPCA to round them up and put them down. The conversation went like this:

Stuart: "Perhaps the reason they don't put the cats down is because it's against their religion". Me: " I think you'll find that religion is not practised by many Sri Lankan cats!" Boom, Boom! Much laughter, and hungry but happy cats left to their own devices.

FAREWELL

Our last night in Sri Lanka was spent at a restaurant called The Tintagel where the whole group enjoyed a very pleasant farewell dinner. I didn't realise then that this would be my last cricket tour. In the following year my sight and hearing deteriorated to such an extent that making such trips, even with the help of my good friends, would be too difficult. These cricket tours enabled me to witness extraordinary events, and experience some fascinating places around the world. I have many great memories and have made new and lasting friendships.

And the cricket was good too

EPILOGUE

Finally, a review of the nine tours to highlight the best and worst of following the England Cricket Team around the world.

"I WAS THERE" MOMENTS

Hoggard's hat-trick in Barbados, April 2004.
My first live Test hat-trick and from a Yorkshire player too. Hoggy was still celebrating the day after the match finished, as he staggered into our hotel.

Lara's 400 not out, highest ever test score, Antigua April 2004.
Great to witness the master recording his world record but hardly edge of the seat stuff, more like numb bum time!

Harmison's first ball of the test at Brisbane that went straight to second slip. November 2006.
What a way to start an Ashes Test series. Never seen anything like it before or since. Unfortunately it set the tone for the whole series.

Sidebottom's hat-trick at Hamilton March 2008.
The reliable Sidebottom went on to take 10 wickets in the match, but we still lost.

Strauss's duck from the first ball of the Johannesburg Test *January 2010.*
It was the first time it had happened to an England opening batsman since the 1936/37 Ashes series. I didn't realise the significance at the time and I suspect neither did Strauss.

Jayawardene scores the 2 millionth run in Test Cricket in his innings of 105. Colombo April 2012.
A class batsman who deserved to be at the crease when this occurred.

HOW DID WE DO?

Played 14, Won 5, Lost 7, Drew 2.

Considering we were away from home, albeit with great support, this was not too bad. There were still people on some of the tours that had never seen England win a Test away from home. It was great to win the first two Tests in Sydney and Barbados. On the other hand, it was very disappointing to grab defeat from the jaws of victory in Adelaide. The win in Mumbai was a surprise as was the defeat in Jamaica. The gripping draw in Cape Town really did have us on edge of our seats.

BEST MATCH

The best Test series was in Sri Lanka. The class of Jayawardene's batting, averaging 88 in the two matches, the outstanding bowling of Swann topped off by the flamboyant batting of Kevin Pietersen.

Colombo was a great victory and the second Cape Town Test was gripping. However my first proper organised tour test in Barbados had a bit of everything. There was Hoggy's hat-trick, Thorpe's ton, Flintoff's 5 for 58 and a win in three days. Add to that the great atmosphere, food and beer. A winner.

At the other end of the spectrum, the England performances in Hamilton, Jo'burg, and Kingston Jamaica were all disappointing. But to declare in an ashes Test with a double century from Collingwood and a ton from KP and then lose as we did in Adelaide was hard to take. Not helped by hoards of gloating Aussies.

BEST TEST GROUNDS

There are a few contenders here. It is tough to separate the top three. Despite its capacity of 44,000 and as the home to other sports such as Rugby League and Union plus Aussie

Rules football, Sydney Cricket Ground (SCG) is still a cathedral for cricket after well over 100 years of Test cricket. Major feats at the SCG include Don Bradman's first class record score of 452, which has since been bettered by Brian Lara (501 in 1994). Today, despite many changes including the rebuilding of the "hill" which used to be the home of a considerable amount of liquid refreshment, it remains a stadium with a lovely balance between old and new.

Despite suffering severe damage from the Boxing Day tsunami, Galle in Sri Lanka remains a stand out home for cricket. The 16th century Dutch fort provides a marvellous back drop as well as a free vantage point which many English supporters took to.

My favourite ground outside the UK has to be Newlands in Cape Town. It has such a wonderful blend of modern stands with great hospitality plus grassy areas and even trees. It has the stunning back drop of Table Mountain and the added benefit of being able to see the Castle brewery and consume its produce. Like Sydney, its Test history goes back to the 1880s and it has hosted over 50 Test matches, disrupted by the national team's ban suffered in response to apartheid that lasted for over 20 years beginning 1970. By the way, my favourite UK Test ground is Trent Bridge which is also a very successful blend of old and new.

The worst test ground at the time of my visit was the Wankhede stadium in Mumbai. The ground was filthy, the security staff unhelpful and seat allocation largely ignored. However the local people were wonderful. Since my visit the ground has, like so many others, benefitted from an extensive modernisation programme. I hope you are now allowed to take your morning paper in with you.

ENGLAND CENTURIES

206 Collingwood Adelaide December 2006
183 Vaughan Sydney January 2003
158 Pietersen Adelaide December 2004
151 Pietersen Colombo April 2012
140 Vaughan Antigua April 2004
128 Strauss Mumbai March 2006
119 Thorpe Barbados April 2004
112 Trott Colombo 2012
102 Flintoff (not out) Antigua April 2004
102 Ambrose Wellington March 2008

Difficult to decide which was the best innings but I will go with Pietersen's 151 against Sri Lanka in Colombo as it set up a win. It was also KP at his attacking best hitting exactly 100 in boundaries (16 x 4 and 6 x 6). His innings of 151 came off just 165 balls.

OPPONENTS CENTURIES

400 Lara (not out) Antigua April 2004
183 Smith Cape Town January 2010
180 Jayawardene Galle April 2012
149 Kallis Cape Town January 2005
120 Taylor Hamilton March 2008
108 Kallis Cape Town January 2010
107 Sarwan Jamaica January 2009
105 Jayawardene Colombo April 2012
104 Gayle Jamaica January 2009

Hard to get passed Lara's world record but it did not lead to a victory on a very flat pitch, It did however lead to a numb bum and my friend Colin's dehydration.

Newlands in Cape Town was the only overseas ground I visited twice. On both visits I saw Jacque Kallis score a century. On the first occasion he scored 149. Although it was not exactly at electric pace as it took over 8 hours. It was nearly twice the next highest score of the match and it did lead to a SA victory. In the same match England struggled to score runs with our number 11 batsman, Steve Harmison, top scoring with 42. Kallis's second hundred was less important in a thrilling draw in 2010.

My choice would be Jayawardene's 180 in Sri Lanka's win in Galle. Although not spectacular it was more than half the total of 318 and set up the win. He also notched a century in his team's defeat in Colombo.

ENGLAND'S BOWLING

Five or more wickets in an innings;

Caddick 7 for 94 Sydney 2003
Hoggard 7 for 109 Adelaide 2006
Sidebottom 6 for 46 Hamilton 2008
Swann 6 for 82 Sri Lanka Gall2012
Swann 6 for 106 Sri Lanka Colombo 2012
Flintoff 5 for 58 Barbados 2004
Anderson 5 for 63 South Africa 2010
Anderson 5 for 72 Galle 2012
Anderson 5 for 73 Wellington 2008
Broad 5 for 85 Jamaica 2009
Sidebottom 5 for 105 Wellington 2008

Ten or more wickets in a match,

Sidebottom 10 for 139 Hamilton 2008
Swann 10 for 181 Colombo 2012
Caddick 10 for 215 Sydney 2003

OPPONENTS

Five or more wickets in an innings;

Lengeveld 5 for 46 Cape Town 2005

Ten or more wickets in a match;

None!

When it came to taking 5 or more wickets the England bowlers easily out performed their opponents. It is remarkable that England's bowlers took 5 or more wickets in an innings eleven times compared to just once by their opponents. Not one opposition bowler managed to take 10 wickets in a match compared to three English bowlers.

The sole opponents' bowler to take 5 wickets in an innings was Charl Langeveldt. He celebrated his success on his Test debut for South Africa. His moment of glory was brief as he only played in 5 more Test matches although he did play in 72 One Day internationals (ODI's) taking 100 wickets, including South Africa's first ODI hat-trick against the West Indies, also in 2005. He went on to become the bowling coach for the Test team.

England's Sidebottom's 10 wicket performance in Hamilton could not prevent a decisive defeat and Caddick's haul in Sydney was in a slightly uncompetitive match. I have to go for Swann's outstanding performance in Colombo with his 10 wickets coming on top of taking 6 wickets in the second innings in Galle.

BEST CRICKET CELEBRITY SPEAKERS

If it was just down to having fun then David Lloyd (AKA Bumble) would be right up there. Like so many of the speakers I have had the pleasure of meeting and listening to, Bumble is just the same when off screen and talking to cricket lovers as he is on the telly. But for all round good humour, warmth and cricket knowledge Jonathan Agnew (AKA Aggers) from Test Match Special comes out on top. When he came to spend time with us one evening in Jamaica he was scheduled to spend about an hour with our group but ended up staying for two hours. During commentary the next day he made a very kind mention of his enjoyable evening with us. We certainly enjoyed it.

Nick Knight deserves a mention. The former Warwickshire and England batsman was relatively new to the broadcasting life and all that goes with it when he came to our group during the Sri Lanka tour. He mixed well and made a good impression with the whole group. It can't be easy being thrown into a group of total strangers and be expected to move smoothly from one small group to another and be engaging, but he managed it well.

BEST HOTELS

If we were looking at modern up market hotels with everything top notch then it would be the two hotels in India (New Delhi and Mumbai). Unfortunately, I cannot remember the names but they were truly excellent both in terms of modern facilities and staff performance.

When considering the setting and uniqueness I would go for Sea Breeze in Barbados. Just writing the name brings back the sound of the sea gently lapping on the shore below my window. There was a perfect private beach, which only Hoggard managed to breach with the help of a jet ski.

For somewhere that is a mixture of a style, modern facilities and wonderful setting, then Jetwing Lighthouse near Galle would be my choice. Situated right on the Indian Ocean, during the Boxing Day tsunami the sea went straight through the hotel, which thankfully reduced the damage. The memory of breakfast overlooking the rocky shoreline in the early morning sun will stay with me forever.

TOUR COMPANIES

I experienced three different specialist companies; Gullivers, Kuoni and The Cricket Tour Company (now called CricTours). I started with Gullivers, as they are a major player and therefore considered a safe bet. They were very professional and I had no complaints on any of the three tours. I can't remember why I switched to Kuoni. When I did we had an issue with their booking process that seemed to issue lots of invoices, leading to some confusion. Kuoni's tour rep also put little effort into encouraging group bonding. To be fair this was not easy with a group about 60 strong.

It was only when we went with The Cricket Tour Company (CTC) that we found our home. A much smaller company but that meant a more personal service provided by people we came to know over the four tours. The ladies we booked with we met on tour; Sue in New Zealand and South Africa and Clare in Jamaica. Even the boss, Brian, would appear sometimes. Their main Tour Manager/Director was the excellent Martin Denyer. An experienced guide as he also worked for the highly rated Journeys of Distinction, Martin went out of his way to make sure everyone was included. For example he would not have seen me out on my own as I was in South Africa 2005. The same people run the business now (Nov 2017) and I am sure they still have a focus on providing a personal touch to a great tour experience.

NEW FRIENDS

One of the really nice things about going with the same tour company on more than one trip is meeting the same people again. John Peck and Richard Birchall met and became friends on a Gullivers tour. They became friends of Stuart and mine when they moved to the Cricket Tour Company. Regulars we met with CTC include Sally and Brian Dow, John Thornton, John and Clare Ward and Julie Spendley. Meeting up with people again makes you feel almost part of a cricket family.
If you want to visit some fantastic places with the cricket being good too, then joining a tour is the perfect answer.

25647133R00077

Printed in Great Britain
by Amazon